A New Spirit in Business

A New Spirit in Business

From
Fear and Need
to
Love and Abundance

Hans Jecklin   Martina Köhler

English translation by
Joyce Brun-Doling
Elizabeth Stocker

iUniverse, Inc.
New York Lincoln Shanghai

A New Spirit in Business
From Fear and Need to Love and Abundance

iUniverse books may be ordered through booksellers or by contacting:

iUniverse
2021 Pine Lake Road, Suite 100
Lincoln, NE 68512
www.iuniverse.com
1-800-Authors (1-800-288-4677)

Cover design by Marco Perini, Switzerland
Original publication: Hans Jecklin & Martina Köhler. Wirtschaft wozu? Abschied vom Mangel. Edition Spuren, Winterthur. 2001 Copyright © 2001 by Hans Jecklin and Martina Köhler Published with the support of E.&H.-Kulturstiftung, Zürich, Switzerland

ISBN-13: 978-0-595-35517-4 (pbk)
ISBN-13: 978-0-595-80004-9 (ebk)
ISBN-10: 0-595-35517-X (pbk)
ISBN-10: 0-595-80004-1 (ebk)

Printed in the United States of America

Contents

Foreword

When I met Hans Jecklin at a seminar at the Lassalle-Haus near Lucerne, I became acquainted with the head of a music company whom I had known both by reputation and from personal experience. In my earlier life as a concert pianist, I had played on concert grand pianos supplied by his company and would sometimes go to his store to practice. I was pleasantly surprised to find the owner of this highly reputed firm at a seminar dealing with global issues from a spiritual and ethical perspective.

However, I was not prepared for the much greater revelation that this book held. Hans Jecklin is not just a manager who is interested in world and spiritual affairs (fortunately, these days there are a number of such people around); he is also an extraordinary person. He embodies the ideal of being both a competent manager and a complete human being—a feeling, thinking, rational, and intuitive person.

This book by Hans Jecklin and Martina Köhler is about the problems of the modern enterprise in the modern world. However, *A New Spirit in Business* is not a sober scientific treatise, but rather an account of a consciousness change through which the new concepts we so badly need come to light. Their book is both informative and autobiographical—and it is a revelation.

Volumes have been written on companies' social responsibility, stakeholder strategy, corporate ethics, and the need for new company cultures and wider visions. This book addresses all these issues, but not as abstract intellectual considerations or even as smart business strategies. It views them from the perspective of a human being who has the courage to ask questions and dares—though often with misgivings that he is honest enough to admit—to take the answers he finds and apply them first to his own person and then to those around him.

In this book, Hans Jecklin and Martina Köhler explore a great many—perhaps all—of the ways in which intelligent, honest, and open people can develop themselves, not for the selfish purpose of becoming richer and more successful, but for the remarkably enlightened goal of benefiting their companies, their families, and everyone with whom they come into contact. This is not altruism—which would be an abstract intellectual attitude—but the recognition that one's own growth is only possible with and through the growth of everyone around oneself and that such growth will ultimately benefit all the collaborators, partners, clients, and stakeholders whose lives are touched by the activity of the enterprise.

Writing a foreword to this book is an almost impossible task. It is too rich, too diverse, too full of humility and daring, fears and courage, introspection, exploration, and action joined with thought. Fortunately, a foreword is not really necessary. Here is the book itself; it can and *should* be read—indeed, there is no substitute for reading it. I can recommend doing so and promise that it will be an experience that could change your life.

We must be grateful that there are people like Hans Jecklin who take the time and trouble to share their thoughts and experiences with us in this way.

Ervin Laszlo
January 2003

Introduction

We first met at a seminar on the topic of economic globalization and the opportunities it offers. Martina Köhler, a journalist, was conducting some research for a radio program. At that time, I was still working as an entrepreneur. We instinctively discovered a common need to understand the present shift in consciousness, to contribute toward making it better understood, and in doing so, to examine more closely a development that calls on us to change, both within and outside ourselves.

In Martina, I discovered a person who perceived the worlds of business and finance from a perspective that was then still foreign to me. A person who had learned early on to be wary of external safeguards and as a result had found faith in simply being. A woman who, already at a young age, had pursued her ideals without first asking herself about the extent of the potential sacrifice. For me, as someone whose understanding of life and external well-being had never been seriously questioned by harsh circumstances, this represented a real challenge—being genuine.

Without this fruitful exchange and Martina's agreement to render it in written form, this book would never have been possible. What was originally planned to be a review and summary of the life of an entrepreneur, developed as a result of our different viewpoints, into something much deeper—mutual reflections about the way in which internal and external change is connected with present-day global economic processes. The work on the individual themes that presented themselves during my journey through life also posed the question of the meaning of our individual existence in the overall context of the community and Creation. Whether commercial endeavors have a meaningful or destructive effect cannot be divorced from the inner values of a single economic player. Our own experiences helped to answer questions about the state of consciousness with which we bring abundance or shortage into the world.

In our part of the world, freedom is generally defined as material independence. However, if this longing for material freedom degenerates to become simply an end in itself and its purpose is no longer contemplated, we suddenly find ourselves dependent solely on material values. If personal freedom really were to be reduced to this level, this would mean that all the affluent people in the world would be enlightened masters—which is clearly not the case.

So where is the meaning and the vision that we—over and above our own personal gain—link with the way in which we act? Since we senselessly shackle an inexhaustible creative potential, this book sets out on the quest to find a way to link inner and outer abundance.

Both Martina Köhler and I are confident that the integration of inner values and external behavior will also lead to new, life-enhancing perspectives in the spheres of business and politics. The responsibility for this process cannot be morally justified. It rather calls on each and every individual to take his longing for happiness seriously and to pursue it far beyond the shallow need for superficial status symbols.

Hans Jecklin

The Vision: A Global Economy
for the World Community

Hans: If we were to regard Creation as a living organism and imagine ourselves to be tiny cells within that organism, I wonder what role each individual cell would play. Their existence cannot be an end in itself, for that would exclude synergetic growth.

Martina: Perhaps life does not serve a specific purpose; perhaps it cannot do anything other than develop ever more complex structures and increasingly differentiated forms of consciousness.

Hans: But then this larger being, of which we are an integral part, also has to take its own course. And that is what arouses my curiosity. In what way does the universe change, and what purpose does my own change—the transformation of one minute cell—have within this creative process?

Just imagine an economy whose profits are the result of the well-being of the community and its environment rather than the lack of it! Imagine an economy whose task and purpose is to produce and distribute goods and services to the benefit of all of humankind, and one that understands profit to be the result of this service rather than an end in itself.

In view of our current empirical knowledge, seen on its own, the idea of an economy that works for the common good may seem little more than wishful thinking. But what if we see this idea as a vision? In terms of time categories, desires are mental constructions, products of the past and present. Visions, on the other hand, are notions from the future.

A vision is always inspiration drawn from the unknown. It points beyond the level where we presently find ourselves and opens up a new dimension of consciousness that is not comprehensible against the backdrop of past experiences alone. Such a transition into a more extensive awareness is not a linear development, for otherwise we would be able to consciously think it. It is a quantum leap within evolution.

A vision becomes reality when our wishes and desires approach the boundaries of our ability to implement them. A vision is the point at which the boundary is transcended. A vision is an expression of evolution and its pulling force. It is, so to speak, the seasoning that gives the soup new flavor, the impulse that is absorbed by the collective consciousness and begins—more or less intentionally—to develop into a trend.

If we can already conjecture that the next leap in consciousness will manifest itself as the ability of autonomous individuals to function as a community, it is because we know that individualism, misconstrued as egoism, has assumed forms that are life-threatening for us all. Experience has taught us that such a leap is preceded by crises and the collapse of old values. But have we not already arrived at such a point? And should we now not ask ourselves which new forms of the community we are already able to anticipate and implement?

In the early 1990s, I produced two videos in collaboration with Swiss television. The first was a recording of choral excerpts from Handel's *Messiah* together with interviews with the Dalai Lama, while the second comprised two television discussions, one with the Dalai Lama and the other with the Jesuit priest and Zen master Niklaus Brantschen, on the theme of Buddhism. In the course of these discussions, the notion of a much-needed directional change in the spheres of politics and the economy was brought up. It was then that I first heard about Brantschen's idea of founding the Institute for Creation of Spiritual Consciousness in Politics and Economy (ISPW, now known as the Lassalle-Institut Zen-Ethik-Leadership).

Filled with enthusiasm for this idea, I wrote Father Brantschen a letter, expressing my eagerness to have new experiences in both my professional and private lives. I offered to work with him at the ISPW. During our first meeting, I became acquainted with the cofounder of the institute, Pia Gyger. She related her experiences in Ibayo, a slum in the greater metropolitan area of Manila where Sister Pia's Greenhouse School, an institution set up by St. Katharinawerk, a Catholic secular institute in Switzerland, was teaching Westerners about new perspectives in global contexts. At the same time, she endeavored to increase the self-esteem and creativity of the slum dwellers. Her account left a deep impression on me, and I immediately decided to make a trip to Ibayo at Christmas with a group from the ISPW.

At that time, I had no idea what I was letting myself in for. I had been forewarned that for a sheltered entrepreneur from Switzerland, such an experience could easily turn into a nightmare. But we were about to move into a large, new house in Autigny, and I felt the need to travel to Asia to view my privileged life from the other side. I wanted to learn something about myself—although I knew neither exactly what it was nor where the journey would take me.

When we arrived in Ibayo, the poverty came as less of a shock than I had originally assumed. Instead, I was occupied with dealing with all the things to which—to put it mildly—I was unaccustomed. For example, we were constantly surrounded by the noise of seven different television channels and the disco and techno music blaring out of a car parked next to our thin-walled hut at four o'clock in the morning. It was never quiet. On top of that, the whole place stank of fish; the local people buy fresh fish, gut them, and hang them up on metal grids to dry. Another even fouler stench emanated from Ibayo's refuse. On the edge of the slum, the city authorities had dug out a huge rubbish pit, to which heavy trucks drove at night to empty their loads. It almost felt as if the trucks were thundering right through our hut. The garbage that they unloaded caught fire and enveloped the slum in dense clouds of black smoke.

In the Philippines, imitation of Western consumer behavior, coupled with a careless throwaway mentality, has led to the costly production of ecologically harmful packaging, which the country is poorly equipped to dispose of. The overcrowded cities can no longer cope with their toxic mountains of rubbish and simply dump their refuse in the outlying districts at the back of the slum, causing countless diseases to spread among the inhabitants.

A shift in perspective causes the character of whatever is being perceived to change with it.

I was shocked. It was also painful, but I was determined to see things as they really were, without averting my eyes. A decisive factor in this was, without doubt, that I felt very secure within the group. Our day was clearly structured. In the morning, we rose in silence, a ritual that was also maintained during breakfast. This was followed by the first of our daily "we rounds," during which we exchanged thoughts and, from the very beginning, examined ourselves from different perspectives: How are things for me as Hans? How are things for me as a Swiss national? And how are things for me as a citizen of the world? I perceived this shift of perspectives as being extremely instructive because the character of whatever is being perceived changes with it.

We met for these "we rounds" several times during the day, as well as whenever we had guests. In the course of these talks, the pain caused by our immediate surroundings was consistently traced back to our own inner suffering, which was reflected all too plainly by the slum. The suffering we experienced as a result of seeing the abject poverty of the slum children made us ask about the inner child within ourselves. And by opening our hearts to our own pain in this way, we were also able to assimilate the deprivation of the slum areas without it triggering an emotional crisis within ourselves.

I was the eldest of the three men in the group. I had taken on the task of cleaning the men's accommodation every day and carried out this work with great devotion and enthusiasm. The men lived in a wooden hut, and we could see the slum through the cracks in the walls. At least the windows had glass panes. There was even a toilet, which, although it had to be flushed using water from a bucket, at least had a drainpipe. If it was not cleaned properly, the cockroaches would climb out of the drain and up our legs. To wash, we stood in the shower and poured water over our bodies using a small vessel, a method I had encountered during my travels in India.

I fetched our water from the communal pump. Seeing a man—and particularly one of my age—performing such work caused great astonishment among the slum dwellers, for the men there seem to leave all the work to the women.

They generally sit around and stroke their fighting roosters; they drink beer or play cards, and many of them seem like wretched ruins. Yet I regard them more as deplorable victims of colonization, particularly the years during World War II when the Philippines was occupied by the Japanese. The crushed zest for life is the worst consequence of all in these former colonies. We knew from experience that by being living examples we might be able to inspire women and young people in the slum to start their own initiatives; however, I perceived a feeling of resentment on the part of the men.

However, we were not in Ibayo to change things for the slum dwellers. Instead, we saw our task as being to support them whenever they themselves took the initiative and began to organize themselves in matters that affected their situation as a community. Our group had not been permitted to take either money or gifts to Ibayo. The intention was for us to experience for ourselves exactly what it felt like to stand there empty-handed. Instead of disassociating ourselves by giving charity, we had no other choice but to simply be there, observe, and communicate. However, it seemed that the most important thing for the locals, too, was that they were perceived in their existing situation. The strength and self-affirmation that arose from this had already instigated a number of initiatives. For example, one group of women founded a food cooperative. Another set up a sewing workshop and now sells its products through St. Katharinawerk. The proceeds flow back into the community in the form of school scholarships or local projects, with those involved deciding how the money should be invested.

In the slum, there are many people who live with anger, strong emotions, and impatience and ardently long to change things once and for all. Once the first sparks of self-esteem and self-responsibility are revitalized and a person rouses the courage to take action, then change is possible. The shift from the victim mentality to the feeling of responsibility for oneself and the community is without doubt the turning point—not only for the slum dwellers, but also for each and every one of us. This feeling of self-responsibility on the part of the individual implies the empowerment, growing out of one's self-confidence, to shape one's own life and to perceive it within an ever broader, ultimately global context. Political consciousness stems from this widening of perception.

We also had deep discussions on spiritual issues within our group. I learned that the nuns of St. Katharinawerk had transcended the traditional understanding of Christ and regarded the Cosmic Christ as the son of Logos and the (female) Holy Spirit, that is, Creation.

When, on Christmas Day in Ibayo, I bent down at some point and touched the ground without really understanding why, it was as if I were touching the Cosmic Christ and, through him, all of Creation. This feeling of oneness with Creation was so overwhelming that it has never left me. I perceived the earth as a living organism and myself as an integral part of it. Since then I have no longer been able to separate—either internally or externally—the slum in Ibayo and the slum within myself.

From what inner deprivations do we create external deprivations? What inner void are we trying to fill by grasping after ever greater gain, power, and possessions? Does the alternative to a world of deprivation not begin within ourselves, by taking our yearning for love and happiness seriously and bringing about within ourselves that which we are seeking on the outside? I believe that once we assume responsibility for ourselves in this way, we will also be in a position to take responsibility for the world.

Whenever I look at myself as a Swiss, I become aware of just how privileged and spared from hardship I am. I have enormous respect for the slum dwellers of Ibayo. While living in community with them, it became clear to me that I could not leave without making some kind of commitment. And I realized that this commitment should not just apply to the slum, but should rather entail comprehending Creation as a whole and, in this spirit, contributing to the well-being of this Creation.

If we regard the earth, and with it ourselves, as a living organism, the slum represents an abscess on this ailing body. However, the cause of this disease cannot be healed simply by treating the symptoms, even though it is necessary to alleviate the pain and treat the wound. A symptom always points to an underlying disharmony in the consciousness of the body. A spiritual healer does not concentrate on the symptoms of an illness; that would merely solidify the energy pattern of the disorder. A healer can only help by perceiving and supporting the implicit harmony and perfection. Only through contact with the essence of our very being do we become an instrument of healing at the deepest level.

In Ibayo it became clear to me that my personal task did not lie in tending wounds but, in accordance with my professional and personal background, in working toward transforming the consciousness in business and economy that lies at the root of these diseases.

A key word relating to this change is *community*. In the film *The Global Brain*, physicist Peter Russell sums this up more or less as follows: We have made this long, evolutionary journey from energy, from the stars, and have now reached a stage in evolution that provides us with a new perception of the way in which we live together on our planet. We have a similar feeling to that experienced by the astronauts when they viewed the earth from space for the first time. From this perspective, they ceased to be Americans or Russians. National borders lost their significance and they felt themselves to be planetary citizens of one and the same earth.

If we understand the history of evolution as an irresistible vortex that unfolds into ever more differentiated manifestations of being, we can see the effects of modern-day globalization, which is accompanied by fear and anxiety, in a new light. Globalization can be perceived as a fundamental expression of the evolution of human consciousness and the opportunity to be an active part of it. It bears witness to a growth that transcends the limitations of nations and peoples in order to enter new dimensions involving our planet and the entire human race. Therefore the possibilities presented by global networking through new and fascinating methods of communication are hardly surprising. However, these new technologies should not be allowed to obscure the spiritual dimension whose material manifestation they represent. Without the link to this background, these state-of-the-art communication systems degenerate into instruments of manipulation employed to maximize one's own interests. But globalization has a much wider-reaching implication—the expansion of consciousness to embrace the global community.

To grasp the concept of humanity and earth as an interdependent organism, we simply need to call to mind the history of the evolution of the universe: according to scientists, this universe began with a Big Bang. In the course of evolutionary development, the light energy that was released combined to form increasingly complex units, from the tiniest elementary particles to atoms, molecules, cells, and organisms, right through to plants, animals, and humans. Man, therefore, embodies the history of the entire universe, down to the tiniest particle in his body. In this sense, each and every one of us is a unique manifestation of this overall, ongoing creation process, into which the various levels of our consciousness development are integrated. Accordingly, the readiness to synthesize and integrate forms the basis of every living being's development.

A newly acquired consciousness dimension opens up fascinating possibilities, which, however, can hardly be implemented without encompassing all the preceding levels. In the absence of the ability to integrate, a purely rational consciousness that excludes feelings and physicality loses its inherent qualities and becomes destructive. To understand this, we only need to look at the way in which our insensitive logic is destroying nature.

> *In a regionalized global economy,*
> *many transport services would be superfluous,*
> *thus reducing the harm to the environment.*

Is it not possible to structure the world economy according to an organic principle of synthesis and integration? A regionalized economy, for instance, would considerably reduce the amount of wasted energy. Many transport services would be superfluous, with the result that significant amounts of energy could be saved, thus reducing the harm to the environment. If we were prepared to calculate the price of energy consumed for transportation purposes based on the detrimental effect it has on the environment, the ensuing rise in the cost of most mass-produced items would result in production being regionalized.

Furthermore, transnational companies would have to reinvest their profits where they were generated. As a result, prosperity, which until now has been concentrated in the industrialized nations, would be distributed globally. The gap between the quality of life in rich and poor countries would be narrowed, and new jobs would be created in developing countries, allowing their national economies to develop in line with their own particular requirements.

Take, for example, the picture of a "family" that is as national as it is global, whose community-driven "relatives" are health, education, environment, culture, public services, and politics. Now imagine an economy that is integrated into this family as an equal member instead of playing the role of patriarch. Would solidarity not be a matter of course? Would such an economy not be willing to have its taxes and levies on profits, revenue, and assets flow into the family to keep it healthy?

Let us stay for a moment with the image of the global family. How can the underprivileged countries free themselves from the shackles of their debts if their imports are hindered by import restrictions imposed by the very nations who insist on free access to the market? And how can a country be expected to recover if its privileged upper strata of society continually deny it the financial resources necessary to do so by practicing capital flight and tax evasion? Resources from which, among others, Swiss financial institutions—and through them, the Swiss economy—profit.

Bosnia, with its 50 percent unemployment rate, is just one example of the gloomy prospects facing developing countries. This country has virtually no large, independent, local production—not even in the food industry, where 60 percent of all consumer goods are imported. And this at prices that, due to agricultural subsidies in the countries of origin, are so low that any attempts to develop production locally are very quickly nipped in the bud. Thus the principle of the free market has totally failed.

It evidently requires considerable maturity to be able to make decisions that benefit the entire family instead of excluding individual members. In his book *A Theory of Justice*, philosopher John Rawls adopts a term used by a four-teenth-century Christian mystic who in his instructions for meditation speaks of the "veil of ignorance". Rawls contends that we must first forget our origin, our country, and our accustomed security if we are to find globally sound solutions. It is only in this state of having forgotten—or, indeed, by donning this "veil of ignorance"—that our preconceptions and desires cease to determine the way we act. Only in the absence of preconceived notions, in a state of being that is completely free of wishes, can we be receptive to being inspired by a vision.

Visions are drawn from the boundless consciousness, from our oneness with everything that exists, from a perfection that cannot be divorced from our own being. Evolution has arranged things wisely by equipping us with an insatiable yearning for this all-embracing consciousness, for that which we call God. With this yearning for ever deeper ways of experiencing our true being, we grow into an all-embracing creativity, whose abundance, diversity, and complexity shapes all of Creation.

> *"Enlightened self-interest"—even the shrewdest of opportunity-minded thinkers learn how to protect the interests of the community.*

While the economy is currently far from aligning its behavior in accordance with this abundance, one trend, which a Swiss entrepreneur once referred to as "enlightened self-interest," has succeeded in asserting itself. The entrepreneur predicted that even the shrewdest of opportunity-minded thinkers in the upper echelons of a company must realize that it is necessary to protect the interests of the community, since their company's existence depends on the well-being of the individual. If fewer and fewer people can afford to buy the products that are dumped onto the world market, or if these products cause our ecological basis of existence to break down, then who is going to buy them? And where is the profit going to come from?

One example of enlightened self-interest at work is the progression of the share prices of sustainability-driven companies, as is documented by the Dow Jones Sustainability World Index (DJSI World). By means of a comprehensive audit, in which nongovernmental organizations such as the World Wildlife Fund and Greenpeace are also involved, the index recognizes the top 10 percent of all listed companies in terms of their social and ecological corporate sustainability. Between December 1993 and February 2000, the rise in the share prices of these companies was 45 percent higher than that registered by other firms. Over the years since it was first set up in December 1993, this index has survived the short-term plunges in prices considerably better than the standard Dow Jones Index (DJGI World; from December 1993 to October 2002, DJSI World rose 73 percent, while DJGI World rose 42 percent).

As a result, an increasing number of enquiries are being made by companies wishing to know the conditions that must be met to rank among the hallowed 10 percent deemed leaders in sustainability by the DJSI. This has led to companies—for once in a positive way—competing against each other for recognition of their efforts to act for the good of the community. Until now, in accordance with the conventional rules of the stock exchange monopoly, shareholders' demands for a short-term rise in prices has enticed managements to maximize profits out of proportion to the original capital invested. This game without limits takes into account neither the environment nor the community. Consequently, a key element of a community-driven, global economic order would be for companies to shift their priorities from aiming for maximum profit to serving the community as the true purpose of the enterprise.

Today, the purpose of an enterprise is primarily limited to benefiting the managers, shareholders, customers, and, at best, the employees. In the future, the aim is to extend the purpose to encompass the well-being of the global community. Naturally, companies will continue to strive for profits; after all, their existence depends on them. Profits are necessary to continually renew companies, to counterbalance short-term financial setbacks, and to pay the owners a risk premium for their invested capital. In fact, many years ago, the Swiss association for free enterprise, the Vereinigung für freies Unternehmertum (vfu), repeatedly stressed that capital invested in a company is committed to a particular purpose and therefore cannot be traded as a short-term convertible asset. It follows that the related responsibility also cannot be simply "auctioned off" on the stock exchange. However, some positive signs of a change in approach have already started to materialize here and there; wherever they manifest themselves, we should recognize the signs and support the protagonists.

Community-driven corporate innovations
- comprise perspectives for a future that is worth living for everyone;
- represent an increase in consciousness, freedom, mutual support, sustainability, nonviolence, equality of the sexes, self-responsibility, and mutual respect;
- contribute toward the improvement of society;
- are easily understood and not dependent on individual people or unique circumstances;
- and prove themselves in practice.

It is the same in our own lives. Sometimes a great many obstacles and considerable resistance are necessary before we are ready to change ourselves. However, evolution does not leave us in the lurch. It acts as a pulling force. Only as long as we resist this force will we suffer as a result of it.

An Indian sage expressed this as follows: "If your actions allow your love to grow, you will know that they are in harmony with the absolute. If they diminish love, then you know that they are separating you from it."

Remembering the Vision

Martina: From our present-day perspective, we are not yet able to describe in concrete terms the vision of a global community in all its various structures.

Hans: It is true that new conditions cannot be created based on old methods. New things do not develop from the models of the past.

Martina: But we are not beings with no history; indeed, we rely on our past experiences. It is important for us to analyze and learn from our past experiences so that we can rise above them.

Hans: Evolution ensures that we constantly rise above ourselves. Our genes are the best example of this. Opening oneself up to a vision does not mean closing one's mind to the past. If we examine our personal gallery of ancestors, we can find signs of our own present-day talents and callings. When regarded as an expansion of consciousness, a vision invariably has an integrative effect.

Looking back at my ancestors, I discover that in every generation there was at least one teacher, one priest, and one organist. Certain elements of each of these professions seem to be perpetuated in me.

Regarding my family's love of music, as far back as 1540 one of my forefathers preferred music to cows. The story goes that he, a farmer from Prättigau, drove his cattle over the mountains to the market in Montafon, Austria, where he intended to sell the cattle and use the proceeds to bargain for two dairy cows. However, he decided first to stop at the local inn for lunch. This decision changed his life, for in the tavern he heard a young tradesman playing a spinet. My ancestor was so fascinated by the sound of this instrument that he persuaded the innkeeper's wife, to whom it belonged, to sell it to him. When he returned home, his wife was not very pleased when, instead of the cows on which they depended for their very existence, he presented the musical instrument, which he had carefully carried on his back across the mountains. From that day on, he spent every spare moment sitting at the spinet. Without ever having been taught a note, he developed his musical prowess to such an extent that before long he was playing the organ in church every Sunday.

Since then, musicians and music lovers have enjoyed a firm place in our family history. My grandfather, Peter Jecklin, left the family farm to study to become a music teacher. He subsequently taught at the Zurich College of Music, the forerunner of the present-day Conservatory. Here, he provided less affluent pupils not only with musical scores, but also with pianos that he had acquired inexpensively. Word soon spread about his special knowledge, and Peter Jecklin became the local expert on acquiring pianos. Gradually his passion developed into a profession. What started as simply helpful gestures quickly grew into a flourishing piano trade. A simple notebook that my grandfather used to record his business transactions documents the date of his very first sale—January 1, 1895. The complete transition from piano teacher to piano retailer took place in 1906. On the death of my grandfather, my uncle took over the business until my father, Paul Jecklin, joined the family firm in 1918 after training as a carpenter and piano builder. At the same time, the business, which until then had dealt exclusively in pianos, was gradually expanded to incorporate both a workshop for string instruments and departments selling radios, records, and sheet music.

That is how it all began. As a result, I was virtually born into the music business. When World War II came to an end in 1945, I was seven years old. In the postwar years, my parents invested all their time and energy in building up and expanding the family business. My mother, who came from a humble background, had married my father against her parents' wishes. Her father was of the opinion that the Jecklins belonged to a class of society in which the daughter of a post office clerk had no place. My mother felt unsure of herself because of her background and from that point onward was continually under great pressure to comply with the conventions of bourgeois society. My two younger sisters and I were also brought up amid this pressure to adapt, for my mother always attached great importance to cultivating good manners. As far as she was concerned, the mastery of such manners determined whether one "belonged" or not. The importance attributed to what other people thought of us was declared to be the key criterion for our self-expression, and rebellion against this code of conduct was the main theme of my youth.

However, without my mother's insistence that I comply with convention, I would probably never have developed the power of discernment that later in my professional life would help me pinpoint and eliminate restrictive rules and regulations. And if now and again I am nevertheless tempted to hold on to conventions, I always end up realizing that the only reliable guide is my own inner wisdom.

For me, personal evolution, and therefore also creative work, mean to continuously identify, question, and transcend rules, which in turn may diminish their significance or provide them with new meaning. Evolution, as a result of the increasingly differentiated structures and more complex interconnectedness that it brings, always goes hand in hand with a greater degree of consciousness and freedom.

Let us, for a moment, regard a company as an adventure playground for adults. From this perspective, the workplace is transformed into a realm of creative experiences in which we become aware of our potential and the new possibilities open to us.

In this vein, I "took over" our music company at an early age. I was keen to help wherever I could and spent every free afternoon there. As my piano playing became increasingly proficient, I discovered that each piano sounds different and that each one can sing or scream depending on how the keys are struck. At the age of fifteen, I could already play very well—unlike one of our best sales assistants, who had never learned to play the piano and was anyway rather hard of hearing. If, on afternoons when there was no school, he had some customers who were interested in purchasing a piano, I would play for them. Naturally—not without some pride—I was keen to demonstrate my piano-playing prowess, until one day the sales assistant said to me, "Play something easy. Then they'll think they'll be able to play it too."

After I had won my first award at a music competition at our school, playing the Sonatina by Béla Bartók, I was occasionally allowed to play for the Hungarian pianist Géza Anda, who in those days was just embarking on his international career. However, my dream of rubbing shoulders with the piano virtuosos of the world was very quickly nipped in the bud. I was seventeen when Géza Anda informed me in no uncertain terms that at my age I should not even consider becoming a pianist if my playing was not already technically perfect. "No one is the slightest bit interested in your emotions. Stop all of this youthful melee when you play," he told me. At that time, I was not aware of the difference between unconscious emotions and more conscious feelings, and I did my best to suppress them both. Yet without a genuine inner commitment to what I was playing, I lost the joy of playing the piano. I was not to regain this pleasure until many years later, when I made music together with my future wife, Elisabeth.

During these early years, I repeatedly encountered various people who impressed me with their outer strength and who stimulated a part of me that wanted to shine outwardly in a similar way. One such person was the classical music producer Walter Legge. Of course, I was fascinated not only by his position of power, but also by his profound musicality and his self-orchestrated, music-oriented life. During my summer holidays, I often sat from morning until night in the London recording studio of EMI (Electric and Musical Industries) and watched Legge at work. Herbert von Karajan once described Legge as "my second musical self." I was full of admiration for the equal partnership between artist and producer when I experienced how skillfully Karajan implemented the ideas that emanated from the control room. Legge's standing in the music world made a great impression on me, particularly because he had built up his position from scratch.

At the end of the 1930s, Legge was working as a music critic. He started his career in the record business writing commentaries on newly released records and was finally appointed senior producer for classical music within the EMI Group. As artistic director of the Royal Air Force Symphony Orchestra, during the war he succeeded in recalling the best musicians in England from their military bases to form an elite ensemble. After the war, under his leadership this ensemble became famous as the Philharmonia Orchestra and, together with the Berliner Philharmoniker, was regarded as one of the finest orchestras in the world. Arturo Toscanini considered it an honor to conduct the Philharmonia Orchestra, while Karajan used it for his first recordings and concert tours. Later, Legge handed over his role as principal conductor of the Philharmonia Orchestra to Otto Klemperer, one of the best-known conductors before World War II, thus enabling Klemperer to enjoy a second, fruitful career at an advanced age. Legge established and furthered the careers of many renowned artists, not least that of his wife, Elisabeth Schwarzkopf, with whom he shared a unique creative partnership. Legge was also the first music producer to take Maria Callas under contract. Both singers starred in opera recordings that remain unsurpassed to this day. In exceptionally rich musical and creative works, Legge set standards that we cannot imagine ourselves being without today.

It was Legge who introduced me to an alternative to becoming a musician. He suggested that he would train me in England with a view to later becoming his successor. The prospect of uniting great power of decision with unlimited creative possibilities as a music producer filled me with enthusiasm, and I seriously considered his proposal. I once asked him how he had succeeded in rising from a run-of-the-mill editorial job at EMI to such an influential position in the world of music. His advice can be summed up in two sentences: "If you have the will, you can achieve anything you want. It all comes down to how much you are prepared to sacrifice." I focused on the idea of being able to achieve anything by having the will to do so—and for the time being turned a deaf ear to the second part of his advice.

A counterpoint to the seemingly unlimited potential of willpower that so impressed me was the inner conflict experienced by my father, who at that time frequently listened to the German Requiem by Brahms. My father's thoughts revolved around the following words: "*Ach, wie gar nichts sind alle Menschen, die doch so sicher leben. Sie gehen daher wie ein Schemen und machen ihnen viel vergebliche Unruhe; sie sammeln und wissen nicht, wer es kriegen wird.*" (Each man's life is but a breath. Man is a mere phantom as he goes to and fro: he bustles about, but only in vain; he heaps up wealth, not knowing who will get it.) My father had a strange affinity for these lines. They touched him in his humility before Creation, a humility, however, that for him was linked with the misunderstanding that he was not worthy of such greatness.

Brahms's words seemed to confirm his feeling that in the eyes of God he was meaningless as a human being.

In contrast to my father's wounded self-esteem, from the very outset my desire for self-assertion was highly developed, with the result that the despair felt by my father somewhat disconcerted me at the time. It was only much later that I understood that he was giving me, with this requiem, a fundamental question to take with me on my path through life: the question of the real meaning of striving for purely material gain. He provided his own answer by making very practical sacrifices. For example, after the war, he was the first person in Switzerland to be offered the opportunity to represent Wurlitzer jukeboxes. In the 1950s, these jukeboxes could be found in every bar, café, and restaurant. My father declined this lucrative offer because, due to his great aversion to alcohol, he did not want to ask his staff to enter public houses to persuade the landlord to install one of these automatic record machines. My father was not prepared to sacrifice his own personal convictions just to make a profit. Is this what Legge meant by "sacrifice"? In any case, I had two extreme role models, and through my various experiences with them I was challenged to find my own way somewhere in the middle.

Whether consciously or unconsciously, we invariably tread in the footsteps of our forebears. However, we decide ourselves whether we want to apply their limitations to our lives or continue expanding from where they left off.

Consequently, nowadays I am able to apply the lines from Brahms's requiem, which my father perceived as being so unacceptable, to myself: "*Mein Leib und Seele freuen sich in dem lebendigen Gott....Euer Herz soll sich freuen und eure Freude soll niemand von euch nehmen.*" (My body and soul rejoice for the living God....Your heart shall rejoice, and your joy shall no one take from you.) In the course of my life, I have become increasingly convinced that I am accepted unconditionally. This has resulted in a positive attitude that forms the creative basis on which, in my own way, I continue the course that was laid out for me by my father.

Once my school days were behind me, and after I had spent some time abroad learning about other companies, at the age of eighteen I joined the family business.

Instead of becoming a music producer, the profession of self-employed busi-nessman seemed to me to be a safer bet. In retrospect, I was pleased that I decided as I did. I learned from the example of Walter Legge how a change in policy in the upper echelons of a record company such as EMI could bring a career as producer to an abrupt end. I also experienced how quickly the music industry's interest in him cooled down when, hurt by this treatment, he dis-banded the Philharmonia Orchestra from one day to the next.

When I was around twenty years old, I fell in love with Elisabeth. We had known each other as children, and although as a teenager she thought I was an obnoxious know-it-all, we somehow came together. At that time, she was attending teachers college, although she already knew that she wanted to become a singer. For days on end, we made music together from morning to night; we started with the first volume of Schubert's songs and did not stop until we had finished the very last one. I can still clearly recall the time we played our songs for Elisabeth Schwarzkopf and Walter Legge. I was proud of our work and was seeking the praise of these two great musicians. Elisabeth, on the other hand, was not concerned with such vanities. She sang because she derived joy from doing so and did not even lose this innocence when I thought I should follow Legge's example and spend hours polishing her interpreta-tions. Fortunately, my actions in this respect did not keep her from marrying me a few years later.

But let us return to the reason for reviewing this chapter of my life. Tracing the past opens up the present. A résumé of one's life reveals a trail of individual marks and proclivities. In short, I can say that the contradictions that were part of my life as I grew up helped to develop my ability to reconcile differences. In my opinion, music is the best example of this, for music continually brings together and unites people from a wide variety of cultural circles.

The musical inspiration of a composer is like visions
that are waiting for us to open ourselves up to them.

The tones of music touch us in their universal essence, irrespective of religion, language, or nationality. The inspiration of a composer to write a symphony is comparable with visions, which merge to form a coherent song for the earth if only we attune ourselves to them. For the composer Ferruccio Busoni, music was the expression of an oscillating cosmos in which millions of songs have existed since the very beginning and are just waiting for us to open ourselves up and listen to them.

However, this opening up does not mean forgetting. The veil of ignorance mentioned earlier refers to our tendency to insist on preconceived opinions and adhere to existing concepts. I can easily recall my opinions and concepts—and for that very reason, I am also able to let go of them again.

I experienced this in a very powerful way in 1999, when, together with a group from St. Katharinawerk, I helped facilitate a peace camp attended by young Muslims, Serbians, and Croatians. Having seen just where the enmity and hate between their parents had led, they were all willing on an emotional level to make peace with each other. As an accompanying team, while we found this emotional willingness important, we felt that it was not sufficient in order for a more deeply based compassion and interconnectedness to be anchored in each individual. Consequently, we asked the young people to split up into small groups and relate their personal stories—the injuries they had received during the conflict, their experiences in the camps, and any encounters with abuse. Listening to each other's stories helped everyone to understand where the narrator was coming from and in doing so to recognize how strongly our actions are governed by the experiences of our ancestors if we are not able to reflect on those experiences. The participants came to realize that it was vital for them to connect their emotional willingness to make peace with recognition of the historical roots of a conflict if their efforts were to have a lasting effect.

In these joint efforts to unfold consciousness, it was not our aim to decide between the vision for the future and the need to come to terms with the past, for each depends on the other. If we remember the roots of our individual and collective backgrounds, we are no longer at the mercy of their effects. Painful experiences cease to cause blockages. Preconceived ideas, behavioral patterns, and judgments that have hindered us from coming to terms with separation and limitations can—once they have been allowed into our consciousness—also be transformed. Subsequently, remembering means more than simply reflecting on the past; it signifies a dawning of consciousness and integration.

An image also presents itself if we take a closer look at the word *remembering* ("re-membering"), which implies connecting again with something that used to belong to us. By remembering, we open ourselves up to all the unpleasant aspects of our life and all our experiences, including those charged with shame, guilt, and pain. Integrating these aspects and experiences means accepting them as elements of our learning and evolution process. We become familiar with aspects that appear foreign to us on the inside—and therefore also on the outside—and recognize them as being a part of our own self. The alien is transformed into the ally.

Modern technology brings even far-flung countries closer together, and as a result, we too move closer together at a consciousness level. It is the pulling force of evolution that, through external globalization, reminds us of the boundlessness of our inner consciousness, and, with it, of the abundance of our being as our true and endless source.

Even though each of us has our own personality and memories, in our very essence we are nevertheless connected with everyone else. We merely need to look back at the history of the universe to find each of us again in the starlight. Evolutionary progress underlines the uniqueness, the personal unfoldment, and the talents of each individual in that it strives all the more profoundly toward becoming united through exchange and community. This seems paradoxical only as long as we are caught up in the "either/or" syndrome. Because the entire history of the universe is contained in every one of the minute particles making up our bodies, we also have a common memory, a common origin. During the act of Creation, the one light—our light—was incarnated into matter and ever since has manifested itself in different experiences or forms of expression. Our uniqueness in the form and our unity in the spirit are mutually dependent. For us to evolve as individuals, we draw on the collective abundance of experiences and forms of expression of humankind. Generally we do this unconsciously, for we are not able to see the field of consciousness with which our thoughts are in constant exchange. At least, we think that we cannot see it, although it is continuously being reproduced on the outside. The material world symbolizes what we think and feel, which is also the reason why we can only transform the world within and through ourselves.

The Synergy of the Strengths

Martina: If inside and outside cannot be separated, the question arises as to the inner economy, the processes through which we grow. What of this new economy is present in you?

Hans: The synergy of the strengths.

Martina: What exactly are these strengths that are supposed to be working together?

Hans: In the field of psychology, one talks of male and female energy. Taking up this image, we can establish that currently the male aspect is overly dominant and is not linked with its feminine counterpart. Our world reflects this inner imbalance and the ensuing deprivations. This disparity is also clearly manifested in the economy.

According to C. G. Jung, the anima—the woman in the man—expresses all the female qualities: intuition, feeling, receptivity, and free access to the unconscious. On the other hand, the animus—the male aspect within the woman—represents rational thinking and active involvement in worldly affairs, as well as the shaping and structuring qualities. Women relate to their inner male in order to give structured expression to their intuition. Similarly, men need access to the female intuition in order to enhance their urge to structure with creative meaning.

In Chinese philosophy, the two complementary, cosmic principles are referred to as yin and yang. They express the polarity in which primordial oneness manifests itself. But how do we bring yin, the female, and yang, the male, into the necessary equilibrium that connects us with the source? How do we bring together heaven and earth? How can we experience these mutually complementing energies as a fundamental strength within ourselves?

I can still recall how, armed with a pair of glasses, a notepad, and a book on organic gardening, I stood in the overgrown part of our garden in Ticino and decided to turn it into a vegetable patch. The ground was rampant with weeds, and in my mind I was already enthusiastically tearing them out. But when I uprooted the tall stinging nettles growing along the dry wall, a huge toad jumped out at me. I had seen the creature on previous occasions, sitting underneath the large-leaved plants in the garden, where it was damp and shady. Now I had unknowingly ousted it from its last hiding place, and, together with the weeds, the toad disappeared from our garden. I had driven away an animal that bears witness to the fertility of the earth wherever it makes its home. The toad also symbolizes the female elemental force. For the time being, however, I had chased it away. Even in my joy of connecting with the female energy, that is, with the earth, the masculine, structuring principle had asserted itself once more.

Within my company, too, I once followed my urge to do away with all the "weeds," that is, the last reserves of disorder and creativity. At the time, our firm owned six CD stores whose managers were given a great degree of freedom to choose the products that were sold in their shops. However, when I found out that at a rival company the entire stock for all twenty-two outlets was managed by a single person sitting at a computer, I wanted to introduce such a system at our firm. The procedure evidently promised an orderly manner of doing business, and I was absolutely fascinated by this prospect.

Without a moment's hesitation, I sat down with my closest collaborator and set about coordinating our stores in a similar way. From behind our desks, we decided that certain music recordings were of poor quality and had no place in a Jecklin shop. We then drove to the various branches, removed from the shelves all the CDs that we considered musically inferior, and replaced them with ones we thought better suited our range. The entire procedure was accompanied by much grumbling and groaning from the various store managers. We were repeatedly met with the same protest, "But that music sells particularly well here." Their remonstrations set us thinking. We spoke to various employees at the "model" firm and discovered that practically all the managers of the twenty-two stores wanted to leave, as the loss of the freedom to determine their product range had also robbed them of the satisfaction they derived from their work.

On learning this, we did a complete about-face. We were determined that the same thing should not happen to us; doing business is a local affair, and store managers should be allowed to decide for themselves what they want to stock, based on the needs of their customers. Luckily, this example showed us what can happen when responsibility and self-initiative are simply rationalized away. Consequently, we decided to give this ability back to our staff.

On the other hand, my radical clearing-up drive in the vegetable garden could no longer be reversed; I had banished the toad for good. With a little more sensitivity, I would have noticed that the ground would dry out if I pulled out all the weeds. Weeds help to keep the garden damp; if you remove them, they need to be replaced with mulch or compost. Here, too, it is a matter of balance, of the synergy of the strengths, because without this balance, healthy growth is not possible.

A male-dominated economy that suppresses female intuition manifests itself in the form of ruthless competition and unlimited growth of everything that is steered by the one-sided fascination with reasoning. If we were to give this structuring, masculine power free rein without connecting it to the receptive female energy, we would inevitably create deficits, and an imbalance would arise. Each organism is kept in a flowing equilibrium by means of a kind of inner communication, with the organism reacting to the slightest impulse. The synergy of the strengths, the way they work together and integrate with each other, acts as an evolutionary principle in each and every organism.

In terms of the economy, expansion of the markets at any cost can be compared to the behavior of a cancerous cell within an organism. Because a cancer cell isolates itself and no longer communicates with the other, healthy cells, it is not conscious of the devastating consequences it inflicts. It is merely attached to its own dynamism; it attacks healthy tissue, forms metastases, and finally destroys the entire organism. Our modern-day global economy is an expression of the inability to communicate with the living world.

The self-isolating mechanisms of the economy reflect the state of human beings, who express their identification with material possessions in increasingly selfish ways. A person who believes that inner need can be satisfied on the outside will grasp whatever he can, without consideration for his environment. He emulates the mechanism of a cancer cell. In the words of the popular Hindu Book of Wisdom, *Srimad Bhagavatam*, "If a person does not have compassion for other people, he can have no compassion for himself, for the same self lives in both."

Communication, which has its roots in the Latin word *communio*, meaning "community," requires that the various strengths work in synergy within our consciousness. I cannot communicate properly with someone from whom I feel myself far removed. As each external manifestation—and thus also each personality—emanates from the invisible, ultimate grounds of existence, I first have to recognize this existence within myself in order to be able to consciously connect to it in the outer world.

In truth, only one source, a cradle of all being, exists. It contains the potentiality of everything that manifests itself in the many physical forms, thus enabling us to recognize the One within the many. Given that oneness appears simultaneously as visible matter and invisible spiritual energy, we have—through our experiences with this apparent separation—an opportunity to develop a deeper understanding of our interconnectedness with everything. To this end, we seem to live in polarity, which includes the constant challenge to reconcile the opposites.

Accordingly, the male and female principles in Creation represent the various aspects of one single being. We are both, and therefore one. If I ignore the hidden man or the hidden woman within myself, I am lacking something, and I project my deficit onto the outer world or onto a partner. However, as soon as that partner rejects this role that I have assigned to him or her, need becomes perceptible. I am in despair. All our relationship problems stem from the misapprehension that one can use one's partner to achieve one's own completeness. Our relationships are characterized by false expectations, assignment of guilt, and apparent deficits. The partner on whom we rely for our happiness is waiting inside ourselves to be brought to life.

My daughters were already in their teens when I came to realize the extent to which I had delegated my female strength to my wife, Elisabeth. I lived my creativity almost entirely though her and her expression as a successful singer. In the classic way, I regarded her as my so-called better half. But then another man appeared on the scene and suddenly this claim of ownership was challenged. I was full of despair, for our conventional, almost innocent, exemplary life was falling apart around us. Elisabeth was taken aback by the intensity of her feelings and I, suddenly so insecure, completely broke down. The sound advice of an old friend led me to a psychoanalyst who specialized in depth psychology. He was an impressive man who was a contemporary of Jung and worked in accordance with his philosophy. He made me realize that I had been vicariously living my feminine side through Elisabeth and was now panicking because she seemed to be distancing herself from me. He helped me to understand that the most certain way to lose Elisabeth would be to try to hold on to her. My need to do this stemmed from the fear of having to give up a part of myself. I had projected my anima onto my wife, and now I had to find and integrate this feminine part of myself into my own being.

Thus I underwent an intensive, inner process, the effects of which at first only became apparent in minor everyday things. I began to work in the garden, and even if I did occasionally scare away a toad or two, I also learned to respect this creature. I devoted more time to my piano playing, which I had neglected for years, and above all I discovered cooking! Cutting up vegetables and consciously feeling what I was holding in my hands turned out to be a real experience for me. When Elisabeth was working away from home, instead of going out with my daughters to a restaurant, I went with them into the kitchen and cooked whatever we fancied. During that time, my children saw me in all my weakness for the very first time. I particularly recall my daughter Barbara, who was then a rebellious teenager. When, during a heated discussion, I told her that I was hurt by her behavior and I allowed myself to shed some tears, our relationship changed. Through this encounter with Barbara, I experienced in a small way that expressing a feeling—even if it is one of helplessness—offered the other person a chance to experience me as an authentic and communicative person. For me, this moment marked the point when we relinquished our roles as influential father and obstinate daughter. After that, we never reverted to our old roles.

Yet before I knew it, with the pleasure of my life energy enhanced by the partial integration of my feminine side, pride at this newly acquired magnitude reared its head. I can vividly recall some of my dreams from that time. I appeared in one of them as the Archangel Uriel in Haydn's *Creation* and heard myself singing: "*Mit Würd' und Hoheit angetan, mit Schönheit, Stärk und Mut begabt, gen' Himmel aufgerichtet steht der Mensch: Ein Mann und König der Natur. Die breitgewölbt, erhabene Stirn verkünd der Weisheit tiefen Sinn und aus dem hellen Blicke strahlt der Geist, des Schöpfers Hauch und Ebenbild.*" (In native worth and honor clad, with beauty, courage, strength adorned, to heaven erect and tall, he stands a man, the Lord and King of nature all. The large and arched front sublime of wisdom deep declares the seat. And in his eyes with brightness shines the soul, the breath and image of his God.) In the dream, I turned around and found Theo Adam, who had sung the part of Adam earlier in the dream, and my wife, who had sung the part of Eve, sitting behind me. They looked at each other and grinned. Although this dream was plain enough, I did not understand what it meant—beyond the obvious humor of my inner self choosing the noted German singer Theo Adam for the role of Adam. So at the next opportunity, I asked my psychologist to explain it to me. He answered with an empathetic smile, "We are certainly divine, but this manifests itself in other ways."

Yet I still did not comprehend what the dream was really trying to tell me. I was much more interested in putting my new powers of attraction to the test. I sought female recognition—and I met precisely the woman in whom I believed I would find it. I floundered through my relationship with her, attempting to play the role of the firm, unshakable rock, which at first I rather enjoyed. The thought that a woman depended on me reiterated—this time in reversed roles—the misconception with which I had previously defined myself through my wife. My masculine self-image continued to thrive on the notion of mutual dependence. However, this time it did not remain unchallenged, for with my newly acquired anima, my intuition also made itself known. It called my old pattern of behavior into question, and I became totally confused.

A helpful therapist suggested that I attend a fasting and meditation course at Lassalle-Haus near Zug, which included two weeks of fasting, silence, and meditation. I had never done anything like that before. Father Niklaus Brantschen, whom I met there for the first time, welcomed us to the seminar. "Go and leave all your problems in the cloakroom. There is someone there who will look after them. Concentrate on meditation and emptiness, and let go of everything else." At that time, I began to realize that I needed an opening to enable myself to deal in a meaningful way with situations that transcended my everyday knowledge. A line in the Lord's Prayer, "Thy will be done," perhaps best expresses what this entails. Meditation opened me up to my innermost, all-embracing self, where everything is connected with everything else, where things I have separated come together again. Some people call this emptiness; others speak of total abundance. But what they are all alluding to is the feeling of inner completeness. This initial—if only passing—experience did not just help me sort out myself and my personal relationships; my recollection of it inspired me to make changes within the company as well.

Every inner evolution that leads our consciousness to oneness inevitably creates a new order of the outer structure connected with us.

The vision of an integral economy means nothing other than connecting male and female, heaven and earth. However, we first need to do that within ourselves. We must be the vision if we want it to manifest itself.

From the Doer to the Shaper, from Factual Constraint to Serving the Purpose

Hans: Yesterday, while playing the piano, I discovered that as long as "it" played, everything was fine. It was only when I started to think about how the piece continued that I immediately lost track of where I was. That reminded me of Toscanini, who once said that he could always visualize the score and each individual part so clearly that he could have written them down from memory. I, however, cannot write down the pieces I play.

Martina: But you are not Toscanini.

Hans: No, and sometimes I am simply careless. I had to empty and clean out the kitchen drawer twice before learning that I should first shut the drawer instead of balancing a full coffee spoon over it.

Martina: Perhaps you cannot be an entrepreneur, a father, and a course leader, memorize music the way Toscanini could, and then try to compete with practical "house-husbands" on top of everything else.

Hans: What or who is it that is chasing me through life?

I call him the "doer." He wants to have everything under control, does not tolerate making mistakes because that would make him feel like a failure, and suppresses his own needs because he does not want to reveal his weaknesses. He does not allow himself to be happy, but he wants to make others happy. He is the inventor of factual constraint, for he strongly believes that things have a will of their own, and he wages war on this constraint day in and day out. For him, there are only winners or losers.

Because he feels small, he is compelled to be the biggest and the best. Everything he does is characterized by helplessness, self-righteousness, and guilt. He attempts to live up to other people's expectations and thrives on their praise. However, it must be said in his defense that in most cases he is not even aware of what he is doing.

It is a well-known fact that there is a world of difference between theory and practice. If I speak on the topic of a just world economic order, I may be asked what I personally have done in practical terms to further this cause. What if I have not done anything concrete and can "only" reply that I have learned something for myself? Do I like admitting that I have not initiated some manifesto or set the ball rolling on a particular issue, that I cannot produce a declaration that has been signed by umpteen economic leaders? Is it easy for me to confess that, instead of running seminars with several hundred participants, I have had to cancel a course due to lack of interest? Does it make me feel good that I have achieved a great deal spiritually but am not able to present any impressive statistics, which everyone seems to find so important? I am repeatedly challenged to rid myself of this burden of having to prove things that has been dogging me for years. Almost all my life I have been concerned with assessing the value of work by its tangible results, and consequently I still find myself reverting to these conventional yardsticks.

After all, as an entrepreneur I was accustomed from a young age to having to validate my actions with sales figures and revenue. And I was proud of what I achieved. Together with my cousin, I was already managing the family company at the age of eighteen. My father, as our mentor, encouraged us to shape and transform the business. We were the exclusive distributors in Switzerland of Columbia, a record label belonging to the EMI Group, and my first task was to restructure and reorganize our sales staff. The ensuing upswing in sales resulted in our firm also being entrusted with other EMI labels, including Parlophone.

Quite unexpectedly, sales of the Parlophone products rocketed as soon as we began stocking them in our warehouses, as the initial releases included the first of the Beatles' many hit records. Of course, adroit marketing and efficient structuring on our part also contributed to this financial success, but in effect all we had really done was to unwrap a gift that had fallen into our laps.

In retrospect, our greatest successes were never the result of cleverly conceived corporate strategies. Instead, they appeared to be guided by a natural flow of energy, which I, as a young entrepreneur, followed more or less unconsciously. This was particularly demonstrated by the following sequence of events.

As the exclusive distributor for Columbia, one of our obligations was to offer a Swiss repertoire. One of our employees brought to my attention three musicians he had heard performing Spanish and South American songs in a nightclub. I invited the three men to come and sing for me. Their music sent shivers down my spine, a sensation I feel whenever I experience something very special. My colleague, too, was convinced that we were listening to something exceptional, so I spontaneously decided to produce a collection of twelve songs with the trio. One of them, "Ave Maria no morro," proved to be a resounding success. We sold well over five hundred thousand records, which at the end of the 1950s was a significant accomplishment.

> *The doer is aroused: he gauges the potential success...*
> *and brings about financial disaster.*

At this point, the doer in me was aroused. I reasoned that if we could be so successful with relatively simple production facilities—up to then we had produced our recordings in a country inn, using simple technical equipment—then surely we would be at least twice as successful if we went about things more professionally. And so, shortly afterward, we were producing, at considerable expense, our next series of recordings by the Trio San José in a studio in Munich, complete with choir and orchestra as well as a professional arranger who had worked with such German stars as Conny Froboess, Rex Gildo, and Peter Kraus and whom we assumed knew how to produce hit records. However, things did not quite work out as I had hoped, as sales of these records were extremely poor. But worse than that, my potentially lucrative journey into the world of "anybody who is somebody" at the Munich music studio transpired to be a financial disaster that devoured almost all of the profit generated by the seemingly simple "Ave Maria no morro."

Having been brought down to earth again with a bump, I decided to listen more closely to my gut feeling when it came to making our own productions in the future. One such project was a series of records for children, which instantly became a bestseller, as did a performance of the nativity story by schoolchildren together with the popular Swiss songwriter Paul Burkhard, who had previously made a name for himself with his hit "Oh mein Papa." In fact, this recording of Burkhard's "Zäller Wiehnacht" is still a popular CD. As it turned out, after that my gut feeling continued to act as a reliable sensor when we had to make decisions relating to our own productions and their economic viability.

Thus I experienced at a local level what happened to the EMI Group at an international level after a high-flying top executive took over its management. The new boss decided that EMI was producing too many flops and not enough hits. In order to cut down on what he considered unnecessary expenditure, he gave instructions to produce less music, and even then to produce only songs with hit potential. Thus his recipe for success was to play it safe, gambling on the notion that a hit was a calculable risk. This business policy ended up permanently destabilizing the group and led to the realization that musical success cannot be predicted in advance.

However, I was a long way off from applying these notions that I accepted in the sphere of music production to my other areas of responsibility within the company.

Almost all of the record labels owned by the EMI Group were represented by our firm—except one. That was His Master's Voice, which was distributed in Switzerland by one of our competitors. When I told EMI's German sales manager that I wanted to represent this label, with a twinkle in his eye he answered with the adage "Complacency makes one reckless." But I refused to give up and traveled to England to talk to the head of the group's export division. I tried to explain that it would be much more efficient for all of the EMI labels, including His Master's Voice, to be represented by one company, namely ours. I explained that we were the right company to do this because we had generated better sales for Columbia than our rival had with His Master's Voice. He listened carefully to everything I had to say. When I had finished he announced that while he agreed with me in principle, he had an even better idea: "We'll do it ourselves. We'll set up EMI Switzerland."

In the long run, there is no doubt that EMI would have set up its own opera-
tion in Switzerland, for, besides the Netherlands, Switzerland was the only
remaining country in Western Europe without its own EMI branch. But now,
thanks to my initiative, this process had been accelerated. When it actually
happened, I was still not able to let go and wanted at least to enter into a partnership with EMI. Thus we ended up owning one third of the company and
transferred our entire sales department to the new firm, EMI Switzerland.
However, I soon discovered that the new joint venture, which under our ownership had flourished and generated profits, now slipped into the red. Already
after the first few months we recorded a loss, a downward trend that was continued to the end of the first year. And so I traveled once again to England, this
time to terminate our partnership. By selling our one-third participation back
to EMI, we managed to get off easily. However, our company had forfeited
approximately half of its sales volume by relinquishing our EMI distributorship agreements, and, having sunk to such a low level, we were forced to
restructure the company and rethink our strategy.

My cousin and I were determined to make good the loss of revenue and pres-
tige. What could we do? At that time, shopping centers were just catching on
and were sprouting up all over the place on the outskirts of towns and cities. In
Zurich, two were in the process of being built. And before anyone knew what
was happening, the rather demoralized doer bounced back again. He immediately set about developing a strategic concept that would enable our present
stores to control the music business in the city center, supported by new stores
in the two "gateways" to Zurich, which would ensure that even customers from
the surrounding areas would not elude us. Unfortunately, the millions of Swiss
francs that we invested in the sales outlet in one of these centers got into the
hands of a general contractor who subsequently went bankrupt. Furthermore,
it transpired that our payments had not been used to settle the various building firms' invoices, with the result that we had to pay some of the bills twice.

Experiences such as these brought my notion of "if I don't do it, nothing will
get done" more into perspective. And I found that the more I followed my intuition, the more the doer retreated into the background, from where he observed
the strokes of good fortune that arose as soon as he relinquished control.

After losing the EMI distributorship, we had built up a wholesale business selling quality hi-fi equipment, but we still lacked an appropriate cassette brand.
During a visit to the Consumer Electronics Show in Chicago, I asked a then-

unknown Japanese firm called Maxell if the distributorship of their cassettes in Switzerland was still available. As the company had not yet established itself in the European market, I heard nothing from them for some time. In the meantime, industry colleagues were raving about their success with Memorex, a cassette that was being marketed as a top-quality product. But it was almost as if we were jinxed; whenever the opportunity arose to make contact with Memorex, I kept missing the firm's head of exports. Then, almost two years after I had first approached Maxell in Chicago, one of its employees contacted us. And I have to say, I did just about everything possible to throw away my chances of securing the distributorship of their cassettes! Unwilling to undergo any risks, I initially envisaged purchasing two thousand units a month. When he heard this, the Maxell representative laughed and proposed that, on his own responsibility, he would deliver ten times that amount. Before long, we were selling one hundred times more than my original suggestion, and sales later rocketed to one million cassettes a month. We became Maxell's best customer in Europe, and occasionally our share of the Swiss market increased to the highest in the world. In the meantime, Memorex rapidly vanished from the market.

And I had done just about everything possible to hinder this development! I had set my sights on Memorex, which turned out to be a product without a future. I couldn't even recall the name Maxell when the firm's employee first contacted us. On top of that, I had acted rather stupidly when proposing the volume of our initial order. After all, they could easily have thought that with my ridiculously low forecast I had no idea about the product or its market potential. Yet none of this did anything to hamper the financial success that we subsequently enjoyed with this product.

The doer is irritated by the unpredictability of coincidence.

How was this possible? At that time, I probably would have answered this question with a simple shrug of my shoulders. My life seemed so unpredictable. This unpredictability irritated the doer in me so much that he did everything he could to keep it under control. Yet simply passing off the entire episode as coincidence would also have meant regarding the existence of every single being as pure coincidence, and thus regarding all of evolution as an arbitrary history invented by a capricious God who gives to one what he takes away from the other.

Evidently we have within us an inner willingness to integrate that drives our evolution forward. We learn and grow based on the circumstances we consciously or unconsciously introduce into our lives. In this respect, our circumstances are not chance happenings, nor are they an arbitrary act of a capricious God.

Nonetheless, I had to admit that it was not any particular business strategy that got us the distributorship of the Maxell cassettes. Nowadays I would describe what was bestowed on us as a stroke of luck. Providence appears to belong to an inner growth that is not always immediately discernible from the outside. This is why we generally experience it as arbitrary, happy coincidences.

Strokes of luck are not triggered by reason, but by intuition. I must have been blessed with intuition when I left my business card with Maxell at the trade fair in Chicago. Everything else was decreed by fate. Strokes of fate, however, impart potential that can only bear fruit when used in conjunction with entrepreneurial skills. Basically speaking, entrepreneurial success lies in this interplay between intuition and practical skill.

While the doer ponders on a solution, intuition hands him one on a plate—though only if we hold the door open to receive it. We do this unconsciously over and over again, with the result that seemingly incompatible events come together to our advantage without us having done anything. Intuitive impulses need to be shaped, not engendered. To shape means to remember, to open ourselves up to the things that are already living within us. The more we consciously perceive this inner storeroom, the more quickly we become willing to draw from it and create. In other words, the doer becomes the shaper.

We had a store in a prime location in Baden that had proved to be a gold mine. At one point, I received a letter from the landlord informing us that he had no choice but to transfer his father's business there. I wrote back saying that in that case I would exercise my rights as a tenant, hinting at the possibility of instituting legal proceedings to extend our lease. I can still picture the enraged expression on his face when he stormed into my office. At that moment, I paused. I suddenly realized I had provoked him so much that he was filled with hatred for me. If this was the outcome of my action, then I was doing something wrong. And so I told him that he should give us notice to vacate the premises when it suited him. My staff were worried and asked me to look for new premises. But contrary to my usual habit, I decided not to do anything. If Baden needed one of our shops, then a suitable place would turn up by itself.

A few weeks later, a customer offered our manager in Baden new premises that were so large our present shop could have fitted into it three times over. The rent was 180,000 Swiss francs per year. My staff were delighted. However, I thought the rent was too high. I also did not want the pressure of having to continually boost our sales, so I instead offered a guaranteed annual rent of 130,000 Swiss francs plus a percentage of our sales volume if it exceeded two million Swiss francs. I was confident that if our cause concurred with Baden's market requirements, a solution would be found. And astonishingly, although there was another party interested in the property who was willing to pay the full 180,000 Swiss francs, the landlord agreed to my proposal. He was not disappointed, for from the very outset the newly opened shop exceeded all our expectations.

In the Baden situation, I consciously heeded my inner wisdom for the first time. I refrained from following my angry impulses and decided to forgo an argument with our landlord. By surrendering my legal rights, I also let go of my fear of losing something, which then eased the situation. As a result, everyone involved benefited. However, things would have developed quite differently had I not heeded my intuition. After all, I had risked losing a profitable business—although admittedly the loss would not have been great enough to threaten the existence of the entire company.

Yet from my experience with the doer in me, I know that even in situations where my existence is not threatened he resists letting go, because he attaches the feeling of security to whatever he is holding on to. He is obsessed with possessing, and when he risks losing something, he feels that his security is being threatened. His inner resistance produces resistance on the outside. But contrary to my earlier feeling of being pressured by circumstances, this time I felt free to decide as I wished. This freedom enabled me to shape whatever impulses I was bestowed with.

The fact that as a success-oriented young man I had been so moved by the song "Ave Maria no morro" might well have had more to do with my yearning for this freedom than I realized at the time. Without my being aware of it, this song had engendered within me an unaccustomed feeling of peace. I encountered this feeling again in Bosnia when, at the farewell party I attended with the young people who had experienced such terrible atrocities, a Colombian singer touched my heart with this melody. Here I experienced the "Ave Maria" as a homecoming, as if I were caught up in one huge intake of breath.

It was only much later that I discovered that it is the natural breath of a piece of music, whether a simple folk song or a symphony by Beethoven, that can bring about this inner harmony. When touched by the essence, the doer can be transformed into the shaper.

I experienced this transformation in a particularly striking way in a Japanese Zen garden. The simplicity of the rock gardens of Japanese Zen monasteries symbolizes the void through which we can become aware of the abundance within ourselves. The gardens' sparseness helps the observers become aware of their inner being. Zen gardens are places of contemplation.

It was therefore an exciting occasion for me when one morning the Zen master Okuda Roshi asked me to rake out the gravel in his rock garden. I took great pains to pull the rake in a straight line so that a uniform, wavy pattern appeared in the fine gravel. Slowly but surely, section after section, I left a trail in the rectangular area of the garden. When I was finished, I called the master. He shook his head regretfully and pointed to the breaks in the flow of the pattern. I started all over again, working even more carefully, more precisely, with more control. But once again, the results of my hard work were rejected. When I set about trying for the third time, Hejiko, the master's wife, who had been sitting silently on the temple steps watching me, stood up. She took the rake from me, drew in a deep breath, and, stepping backward as she slowly exhaled, lightly and fluently traced a long trail in the gravel. Then she indicated that I should do the same. By following her example, I became conscious of my breathing, and the more I linked the movement of the rake with the rhythm of my breathing, the more harmonious the pattern I left behind me became.

The master noted what I had done without any further comment, just as how, a few days earlier, he had observed how I had carried out the task of clearing up a part of the garden without any sign of acknowledgment. The doer in me missed the praise of the master even more intensely when, on the last day of my stay at the monastery, I handed Okuda Roshi a generous donation. Without opening the envelope, the master passed it to one of the monks. Although I knew that my desire for praise was rather petty, it was clear that I still needed to examine this emotion more closely. Finally I came to realize that giving and receiving complement each other, just like inhaling and exhaling, just like the waves in the gravel in the Zen garden.

If we had to breathe the way we do business,
we would have run out of breath long ago.

In terms of the economy, too, we depend on being able to entrust ourselves to the natural balance produced by breathing and act in harmony with its rhythm. If we had to breathe the way we do business, we would all have run out of breath long ago. By generating profits, the economy may well be breathing in, but it does not breathe out sufficiently to keep the organism healthy. It holds its breath, so to speak, and at a global level this imbalance is now threatening to take our breath away altogether. If our actions follow the undisturbed flow of our breathing, they also link that within us and that outside in a natural rhythm. We shape. Once we have balanced the male and female aspects within ourselves, giving and receiving flow into each other. The unfortunate doer falls out of step with this rhythm and assumes a manner of behavior focused on material security and based on one-sided taking. He is so obsessed with the things on the outside that finally he is ruled by them. So-called factual constraints now govern his way of acting. When we look at job advertisements for top executives, the heroic ideal of the doer is omnipresent. It is therefore hardly surprising that much of the economy is ruled by doers, who soon find themselves victims of growth rates and share prices, that is, victims of factual constraints.

Of course, one could argue that my management experience is limited, as the competitive pressure in the music business—and in a relatively small enterprise at that—is not the same, or in any case is less fierce, than in other areas of business or large corporations. While that may be true, the mechanisms that create the illusion of factual constraints are based on the same thing whether they occur in large or small firms.

Through our Swiss distributorships of EMI and later of Maxell, I discovered in concrete terms how the pressure exerted by international corporations to step up sales can trigger a series of chain reactions. Whenever I had to negotiate the sales budget for the following year with Maxell's export manager for Switzerland, I found myself sitting opposite someone who was expected to increase his customers' sales quotas by a couple of percentage points each year. But at some point our market share in Switzerland had reached 40 percent and more, and we realized that anything over and above that would not be healthy. We did not want to arouse opposition that might spark cutthroat price wars. While such rivalry might result in a short-term growth in sales, at the same time the profit for everyone involved will inevitably shrink, with a long-term tendency toward zero. We had also discovered that customers see a product as less valuable if it is sold at dumping prices. Consequently, the high regard for the product that we had built up over a period of years was now at risk.

However, when the three major Japanese cassette manufacturers, Sony, TDK, and Maxell, were no longer able to boost sales any further because the quality of these products had now reached the limit and CDs were already setting new standards in the field of sound quality, they then started to build new factories in Europe. How absurd! In view of the declining market, all three major players were now expanding their production capacity with the notion that by reducing production costs, they would increase their market share to the detriment of their competitors. Of course, this logic proved to be fallacy. The shift from quality marketing to price marketing led to the factual constraint of volume growth, which resulted in everyone's profits plummeting.

The self-made pressure to put huge volumes of cassettes onto the dealers' shelves became so intense that the companies ended up selling the cassettes at dumping prices. The three rival companies, now suffering from overcapacity, continued to turn the price/volume carousel round and round. Products were sold at ruinous prices, and when one of our biggest customers said to us, "Right now your Maxell cassettes are cheaper in Germany, England, Belgium, and Hong Kong," we, too, were continually forced to cut our prices. Before long, we were selling the cassettes at purchase price, until in the end no one wanted to buy them from us at all because they could be had even cheaper elsewhere. Finally, there was no profit whatsoever to be reaped from the sale of these products, and so we withdrew from the wholesale trade in cassettes.

The principle that a top-quality product should have its price and that the volume produced should correspond with the demand had been totally disregarded. By becoming a throwaway product, the cassette had been deprived of its significance as a service for which the customer was ready to pay a fair price. In the end, the fulfillment of the original purpose of the product bowed to the supposed factual constraints known as the battle for market share.

The following story also took place in the same context. One of our biggest customers was an avid supporter of Maxell cassettes, and this company profiled itself with low prices. A former senior employee of this firm had set up on his own. He owned a small rival company and wanted to get back at his former boss by selling Maxell cassettes at an even lower price. The two ended up entangled in a never-ending price-dumping spiral. Of course, in the meantime our sales figures rocketed. However, I could clearly see where this game was leading: not only the two rival firms, but also our two thousand other retailers, would soon be making no profit at all on these cassettes. The product ran the risk of losing its value. Consequently, I wrote the feuding parties a very frank letter expressing my concern and urging them to bring this destructive game to an end. And surprisingly enough—more quickly than I could ever have imagined—they did agree on a truce.

However, totally bent on my desire to resolve this situation, I had not taken into account the side effects of my efforts. Once the price war had come to an end, our cassette sales shrunk back to their normal level. However, since we ordered our supply from Japan three months in advance, all of a sudden we found ourselves sitting on almost a year's supply of Maxell cassettes. This stock needed to be not only financed but also stored.

What did I learn from this episode? I had also fallen into the trap of factual constraint. After all, I had been so engrossed in stopping this price carousel that I had failed to consider the broader impact of my actions. While I brought the price war to an end, I forgot all about my own stock of cassettes. Had our company not had sufficient liquid assets, those three million cassettes could well have resulted in serious solvency difficulties. In other words, I learned that when I want to settle a crisis, I must not become engrossed in it. If I concentrate all my energy on the problem, I merely strengthen it, narrowing my perception and causing myself to overlook integral solutions.

Although one might least expect such problems in the army, even here one is aware of interrelations such as these. Ironically, the military apparatus is the organization in our social system that is most distinctly encumbered with fear and prejudices. I recall one particular lesson in tactics while I was serving in the Swiss army. Our exercise involved a village that was occupied by the "enemy." As trainee officers, we were given the task of drafting three platoon sections comprising around thirty soldiers to "recapture" the village. We agreed that we should send in one group from the left and one from the right and hold the third in reserve. "Say the group on the left gets through, but the one approaching from the right is blocked," our instructor said. "Where would you employ your reserves?" "On the right, of course, where the attack is blocked," we replied. The instructor laughed. "No," he said, "at the place where they are making headway."

In many areas of life we can observe that we tend to invest more in bottlenecks and deficiencies than in qualities and strengths that are already bearing fruit. Investing in the latter means following the path of life.

The story of a young man who had inherited his father's rope-making business is a small, positive example of the courage to open oneself up to the opportunity presented by dwindling business. Due to the decreasing demand for handmade hemp rope, the production costs were no longer in proportion to the demand. At first, it looked as if the young entrepreneur would soon have to close the business. But then he had the idea of producing decorative wall hangings that could be used to tie back curtains, affix lamps to a wall, or attach flowerpots to house façades. He started to specialize in this field. Since then, he has been supplying handmade wire rope in a range of gauges all over the world, along with wall hangings that are not just practical but attractive too. This innovative businessman had accepted the limited profitability of his family business instead of desperately trying to survive by continuing the old production methods. By letting go of the old, he opened himself up to his intuition and was receptive to new impulses. Thus he discovered a niche in the market that linked his products with business profits.

Of course, it is far from easy to keep a clear head and an open heart when we find ourselves in situations that trigger fear. This requires inner distance—and who has that in a crisis situation? In cases such as these, a Zen teacher was accustomed to posing the following questions: What does your problem have to do with eternity? Would your decision make sense from the perspective of the last minute of your life? Such questions cause us to stop and think, and perhaps can help us out of the never-ending circle of notions and emotions surrounding a particular problem.

To have the courage to make the leap from serving factual constraints to serving the purpose and from being the doer to being the shaper, we find that one question helps us focus our actions: *Am I acting out of love or fear?* We have all experienced the fear of failure, the fear of losing our status or position of esteem. The more we repress these feelings, the more intensely the outcome of a crisis will be determined by this fear. If, refusing to listen to reason, we attribute our actions to supposed factual constraints, we are refusing to take responsibility for our fears. Yet if we do not accept our own fears, then who will? Our work colleagues? Those around us? Society? Only when we become aware of the fear within ourselves, and accept it instead of repressing it or projecting it onto the outer world, are we set free to shape things.

It requires courage, and it also goes against our social conventions, to assume responsibility by recalling the consequences of our actions and changing the deeper causes within ourselves. By doing so, we stop judging both ourselves and others, and we start to develop compassion for ourselves and our environment. Accordingly, the ability to feel compassion is perhaps the most truthful reference point that we can rely on to guide us on the path to integral consciousness.

Looking back over my life, I realize that there were various stations along the way that helped intensify my contact with the shaper in me. One of these was my encounter with kinesiology. I learned this technique of balancing the energy in the body from one of its most creative pioneers, John Diamond. By means of this methodology, Diamond enabled me to experience the correlation between music and life energy. I first met this American psychiatrist and music lover in the 1980s. One day, after one of my business colleagues had told him about me, he turned up unexpectedly at my office. At first, I received this unannounced visitor with rather bad grace, but today I am glad that out of curiosity I decided to listen to him. From him, I learned why it does not depend just on the piece of music itself whether the listener's life energy is strengthened or weakened. Diamond showed me the relationship between the natural flow of breath of a composition and that of the musician and taught me that whether the inherent life energy of a composition will reach the listener depends on the musician's ability to tune into the pulse of the music. By showing me the reactions of my own diaphragm as well as using kinesiological tests, he demonstrated to me the effects of different compositions in connection with their interpreters. If performers attune the pulse of the music to their own, the listener's diaphragm stretches when he or she breathes and the muscle tone increases. Otherwise, the listener's breathing becomes restricted and the muscle tone becomes weak.

In the introductory seminars and workshops led by Diamond, professional musicians and music students had the opportunity to have the same experiences. The effect of the energy transmitted by the musicians was not correlated with conventional musical yardsticks such as mastery of one's instrument or musically correct interpretation. Even musicians who played the piano badly but were at one with the inner pulse of the music were able to enhance the life energy of the audience. The fact that musicians sometimes block their life energy and consequently that of their listeners may simply be due in part to the unnatural body posture that musicians tend to assume. There were violinists who simply needed to relax the wrist of the hand holding the bow to connect with the energy flow of the music once more. Conductors experienced the enhancing effect of their gestures on both their audiences and the musicians themselves, and, of course, also experienced how draining music could be when their movements no longer harmonized with the natural pulse of the music. Choral conductors have a greater tendency to relate their gestures to the pulse of the music because they are used to breathing along with their singers and thus inspiring them.

Harmonizing oneself with the natural breath of a composition in this way means more than just reproducing it in a technically perfect manner. It means connecting oneself with the power from which, as Johannes Brahms once expressed it, "all truly great composers drew their inspiration....We call it God, Omnipotence, Divinity, the Creator, and so on. It is the same power that created our earth and the whole universe, including you and me." Does this not apply to all areas of life? Are we not capable at any given moment of connecting our actions with this power?

Diamond's experiments made one thing in particular clear to me: if a musician feels stressed by the pressure to perform well, or if he or she wants to shine by means of particular virtuosity, this means that the musician is fixated more on the success of the performance than on the pulse of the music. Thus the playing loses the love, joy, and freedom that make music such a magical experience in the first place. This lack of inner freedom is translated to the audience in the form of depleted life energy. The performer detaches the music from its breathing pulse in the same way as he cuts himself off from his inner strength. His playing literally has a "breath-taking" effect.

Through my experience with kinesiology, which allows the muscles to "speak," I realized for the first time what an enormous influence it had on my surroundings whether I expressed myself as a doer or a shaper in my thoughts and actions. Even if these effects do not manifest themselves clearly, they are always present in the form of life energy and exert control from the background.

John Diamond's work has contributed greatly to an understanding of music that stems from the knowledge of harmonics dating back a thousand years. Though subsequently our ways parted, I was convinced by his findings and devoted myself to making them better known. Among other things, I arranged to have his book *The Life Energy in Music* translated into German and found a publisher willing to copublish it with me. This book has sold many copies and has been read countless times. I do not think that I am imagining things when I say that, since Diamond appeared on the music scene, I have read an increasing number of concert reviews about musicians who play in accordance with the inner pulse of the music. This may be because critics have developed sharper ears, or perhaps a new generation of musicians is now emerging that is succeeding in integrating the breathing rhythm into their music.

This revelation opened up a new perspective for me. Every form of musical expression that truly springs from life energy will transport us, so to speak, into its pulse of breathing, into the harmony between the inside and the outside, the harmony between body and soul. The message conveyed by a composition that draws on infinity in this way has a therapeutic effect on our entire life energy system as soon as the musician transmits it by playing. Once again I recognized the real meaning of my work as a music retailer—to promote and make available the healing power of music.

In the course of my kinesiological training with Diamond, I naturally also recognized what kind of music intrinsically lacked this source of inner strength. For example, I discovered that certain genres of rock music evoked violence and self-destruction instead of increasing life energy. These days it is well-known that sound designers in the music and film industries work with sound frequencies that our ears cannot hear but that nevertheless have a manipulative effect. When I proved this to my staff by means of an experiment, I was met with anger and opposition. It was clear to us all that withdrawing certain hard rock productions from our stock would mean the end of our CD stores.

This put me in a quandary. On the one hand, I wanted to fulfill my desire to serve the well-being of our customers and enhance their life energy, but I also did not wish to jeopardize our business. At the same time, I asked myself to what extent I was entitled to censor the wishes of the customers. Faced with this "either/or" conflict, we managed to find a way around the problem. We decided to surround the hard rock CDs with alternatives such as blues rock and anything else from the range of world music that, like all compositions that draw their impulses from folk music, has an energizing effect. At least in this way, the occasional hard rock fan might "accidentally" have a more life-enhancing listening experience and thus hear the difference from the type of music that arouses aggression.

I had made a decision in which out of a rigid "either/or" position had come a "both/and" solution. However, I did not feel entirely happy about the fact that I was still not doing full justice to the standards I had set for myself. Was I allowing myself to be influenced more strongly by my desire to prevent a drop in sales than I wanted to admit? Yet what was so wrong about also wishing to serve the interests of the company? Over and over again, I confused my yearning for unity with one-sidedness. I wanted to be good instead of whole, and I had difficulty accepting both the doer in me and the fact that there are customers who actually prefer hard rock. After all, their preference does not necessarily mean that these customers close their ears to other types of music. In the end, my inclination to take responsibility for other people stemmed from the fact that I was judging their needs. I was on the verge of depriving them of making their own experiences.

A Hindu scholar later gave me the following advice on how to deal with this recurring conflict: "With the light of your heart, you have the gift and the possibility to free people from their entanglement with extreme darkness. But do not think of, and certainly never even try, transforming the extreme darkness, for this darkness is also an expression of the One, and in order for Creation to continue, it needs the counter pole to the brightest light. At some time the darkness will be transformed, but that does not lie in your hands. The time for an end to the material universe has not yet come, and as long as the present Creation exists, it needs polarity."

Without polarity, we would not have evolution. I can only know about the shaper in me because I have also experienced the doer. Polarity as a basis of experience helps us to understand who we really are: male and female, heaven and earth. Our path to integral consciousness is not a path of either/or, but rather of both/and. It comprises change, not resistance.

During one of my stays at an Indian ashram, I considered the question of how I could rid myself of the doer in me—of whom by this time I was only too well aware—without being branded as a dreamer in a world that required me to act. I was standing in the queue to get my lunch when a monk came up to me. "Are you Hans from Switzerland?" he asked. When I confirmed that I was, he placed a small, folded piece of paper in my hand. "Non-doership does not mean inaction," it said. "It means action without anxiety about the result. How can that be? It is because, having done your best in a situation, you are surrendered to whatever result God wills. You know the result you are aiming for. As best you can, you design and carry out actions to get you there. While you carry them out, you do not worry about the outcome, what it will or will not be. Having done your best, you accept the result. It is God's will for the situation."

The Vision as a Fundamental Wave within the Enterprise

Hans: From the very beginning of our joint management of the company, my cousin and I embraced one particular guiding principle:"The size of our enterprise should not exceed the scope of our hearts."We have always fared well with this maxim. I do not believe that a company's meaning that has been determined by the management alone can flow through all the various levels to the customer without being diluted along the way. The longer the path, the less remains by the time it reaches the end.

Martina: In that case, it seems justified for managers of large corporations to simply give in and say,"I don't know my numerous employees any more than I know my customers.What use is all this fuss about a meaning if it cannot even be relayed properly?"

Hans: There are no limits to the way a meaning can be relayed. Limits only exist if the essence of the meaning does not contain a great enough force of attraction, and if the notion governing the growth of the company is limited to multiplying external structures that are controlled by centrally instigated regulations. Here, stronger motivation and increased "conductivity" within the corporate structure are required to prevent the entrepreneurial impulses from getting bogged down in the various spheres. However, this cannot be achieved by means of regulations.

Martina: How then can we increase this "conductivity"?

Hans: By means of a vision borne by all the employees.

At the beginning of the 1980s, I felt, for the first time, the need to draw up a corporate mission statement, so I sat down with our advertising consultant to draft something suitable. In order to elaborate my personal attitude toward the company, we created a nice little chart with a picture of a conductor swinging his baton. The conductor was supposed to be imparting the mission statement. This statement included four attributes we decided should characterize our company: professional competence, helpfulness, vitality, and a close affinity to music. In addition, there were four performance criteria against which to measure ourselves: product range, professional competence, service, and competitive prices. In terms of our corporate policy, we at least declared our intention to act in the service of the public, both by making music available in its many forms and by renouncing excessive growth. We intended that the enterprise should continue to develop within the framework of its social and economic environment, in a healthy and harmonious fashion.

A few years later, I decided to adapt this mission statement in line with changes that had occurred within the company. Our new advertising agency recommended the communication consultant Edmond Tondeur as an experienced adviser. I asked him to draft a new version of our mission statement and told him what I thought it should include. To my surprise, he turned down this assignment, declaring that a corporate mission statement could only be conceived collectively, in collaboration with our employees. However, he agreed to assist us in our endeavor in whatever way he could. Thus, in October 1988, we drove with twenty departmental heads to the Rigi mountain in central Switzerland, where we spent three days working on our new mission statement. Several more such sessions followed and subsequently, regardless of where they were actually held, went down in the company's history as the Rigi sessions.

To kick off our first mission statement session, I used a text from Antoine de Saint-Exupéry's *The Wisdom of the Sands* that expressed my feelings exactly: "If you want to build a ship, don't drum up the men to gather wood, divide the work and give orders. Instead, teach them to yearn for the vast and endless sea."

Not used to first feeling my way toward a specific goal and then imbuing it with spirit before implementing it, I nonetheless felt the truthfulness of Saint-Exupéry's words—and was disappointed that they failed to trigger any response from the group. My notion of euphoric employees working at a euphoric firm also suffered a severe blow on the very first day: the entire team used this opportunity to give free rein to all their discontent relating to the company. I was like a cat on hot bricks, anxious to immediately provide each critic with an appropriate answer. However, Tondeur, my adviser, held me back. "Just listen to what they have to say," he told me. "It's important that they get all of this out of their system. Besides, you don't have to have an answer for everything." Yet that is exactly what I did want, as I was eager to emerge from the work session as a ruler of minds. I must admit that I needed several more such sessions before I was capable of working together with my colleagues and before I understood that the freedom to express anger and criticism is indispensable if we are to make room for something new. Later, I wrote in a personal addendum to the session: "We draw on the things we like to do best because they give us pleasure, on limitations because they make us creative, and on our deepest yearnings because they lead us to the source of our very being."

However, everyday life at the company soon revealed that it was not so easy to deal with limitations as I had predicted in my notes at the time. All the same, our first jointly drafted mission statement contained fourteen statements concerning the internal dialogue as regards our customers, our employees, and the sustained existence of the company. We agreed that our mission statement should be neither a set of rules of conduct nor a list of strategic goals. Nor should it be an imposing self-portrait that did not do justice to our everyday business life. We wanted a mission statement to which we as individuals could align ourselves within the enterprise and toward which we could gear our actions. It should be a mirror of our strengths and weaknesses, a basis for a self-confident manner of working, and a basis for the development of mutual trust in our relationships. We regarded the implementation of these things as a process. The departmental heads kept notes of their experiences and shared them at regular intervals. Thus we were able to clearly identify the difficulties that arose in practice.

Time and time again, I felt that the criticism expressed by our employees hindered me. Whenever there was talk of too much pressure to perform, of too much hierarchy, of too little leeway to act independently, or—in connection with the not-particularly-attractive salaries paid to the sales staff—of a lack of job satisfaction, this aroused in me a mixture of opposition, despondency, and the urge to take flight. Such criticism, however, was simply an integral part of the constantly growing exchange within the company. And as we set about implementing the mission statement, my willingness to change also grew. I learned in a particularly striking way just how productive it ultimately is to take employees' reservations seriously. Only by addressing these reservations was I able to discern whether they contained any fundamental messages that necessitated a change in direction or whether they stemmed from a fear of change.

Fear is nothing more than blocked creative energy. It begins to flow again as soon as it is met with acceptance instead of impatience and actionism. Thus I gradually learned how much creative potential lies in circumstances that are ostensibly experienced as restrictions and is set free as soon as we address these circumstances. Numerous Rigi sessions were devoted to staff development to enable us to achieve our creative potential together. The issues that these sessions brought to light provided us with material for a process lasting several years, during which we discovered how to create conditions that enhanced the employees' enjoyment of and satisfaction in their work, rather than stifling their valuable motivational energy. Instead of dwelling on shortcomings as before, I learned to identify and focus on the potential of the individual employees, as well as on the potential of the teams. Moreover, this shift of attention from supposed deficiencies to the positive qualities of those around me also had an effect on myself; it encouraged me to practice accepting my own shortcomings in the same way. In my notes of the time I wrote, "If everyone occupies a position offering challenges that fill him with joy, his energy can flow freely to where it is needed."

A series of seminars with the title of "Joy in Serving" that were organized along these lines initially met with opposition, as the concept of serving is usually associated with a difference in status between the person serving and the person being served. This misunderstanding sparked many productive discussions. For example, when asked by the course leader what gave him the greatest satisfaction when dealing with customers, one employee replied, "Whenever I can prove to the customer that he is wrong." Evidently, as a provider of services, this employee did not feel himself to be on equal terms with the customer. His statement confirmed the need for our seminar, as its objective was to strengthen the self-confidence of the participants and promote an understanding of a concept of serving that aimed to enable employees to experience themselves on equal terms with the customers. On this basis, they were able to reappraise their own qualities, such as professional competence, patience, and an ability to communicate, which in turn gave rise to increased satisfaction both with themselves as human beings and with their work.

Of course, this process did not always run smoothly. For example, we had agreed that every week each sales assistant at our CD stores should give away a free CD to a customer they felt would particularly appreciate it. Many of the employees had inhibitions about doing this, as they were afraid that the customer might view this gesture as an attempt to curry favor. Once, when I met Claus-Helmuth Drese, the former director of the Zurich Opera House, he said to me, "It's amazing at your stores. Whenever I step through the door, I'm presented with a CD as a gift." Our sales staff tended to assume that a prominent patron would not misunderstand their gesture. Furthermore, it appeared that they repeatedly made gifts to customers with whom the ice had already been broken, which was obviously not the original intention of the exercise.

The self-confidence of the individual repeatedly proved to be the be-all and end-all within the work processes and, as an entrepreneur, I sought all kinds of ways to boost our employees' self-confidence. On one occasion, quite by accident, I came across an American course program called "Color Me Beautiful." It is based on the knowledge that the skin reflects colors in ways that either enhance or diminish our charisma. Based on Goethe's theory of colors, each tone has four characteristic shades that radiate various degrees of warmth or coolness and can be associated with the seasons of the year—spring, summer, autumn, or winter. The aim is to help people find the family of shades that enhances their own particular skin type. I participated in such a workshop together with one of our female store managers. I can still picture her shining eyes as she stood in front of the mirror and discovered how much prettier the appropriate shade made her. I wanted to offer our staff this small pleasure and witness the change it brought about inside them. From apprentice to manager, it had the same beneficial effect. And I discovered how important the staff's self-esteem is to the successful development of a company.

Another initiative within our mission statement process was our cultural program. The employees were motivated to attend cultural events of their choice by being able to receive from the company a contribution toward costs. While there was no ceiling on the number of events, the offer was only valid if at least three events were attended per quarter. This program proved to be an ongoing success. Our employees attended concerts, theater productions, and opera performances that were of particular interest to them, and they shared their experiences with each other, as well as with the customers. Furthermore, their presence at the events generated a positive response among musicians and regular customers, and furthered our endeavors to network with the local music scene as stipulated in our mission statement.

One outcome of these changes was that at the beginning of the 1990s my cousin and I decided to restructure the company. It was our intention to withdraw from operative management, and as our children were not interested in taking over from us, we developed a ten-year plan to make the company less dependent on us. We realigned the former owner-oriented, hierarchical organization to create a corporate structure that resembled an arrangement of intersecting circles. During these changes, we also introduced our—as it later transpired, temporary—successor to his various duties. This step entailed a great deal of responsibility on our part, and I was far from certain about the future of the company. When, in the course of these developments, I read Matthias zur Bonsen's book *Führen mit Visionen* (Leading through Visions), I immediately knew that his approach would bring us considerably further.

A vision is not made. It is already there,
just waiting to be discovered.

In view of our plans to restructure the company, I quickly succeeded in persuading both the management and the board of directors to attend a workshop with the author of the book. During our work with him, we realized that a vision is not made, but rather discovered, because it is already present in the collective consciousness of all the members of the company. This insight took us straight to the next step. Until then, this topic had only been discussed among a relatively small group of management staff, so we now decided to repeat the workshop with all 150 employees participating. Despite the uncertainty as to whether my and my cousin's ideas—which were easy to present to a small team—might go under in a large group, curiosity compelled us to give it a try. We both agreed on one thing: the company should be guided into the future by a vision that would be discovered by us all.

As we could not simply close our stores for several days in a row, we worked for two days with half of the staff, followed by another two days with the other half. In both small groups and plenary sessions, we pinpointed and discussed the values that had been drawn up and were to be developed by the company to the benefit of society and our customers, employees, suppliers, and investors. We learned to perceive and express our inner visions. When the entire staff met on the following Sunday to compile all these images, we were surprised to discover how much we agreed on in terms of the meaning and the values of the company. This shared meaning is what gives a corporate vision its power, for it is instilled with energy by the entire workforce. Through this collective process we learned that a vision is not merely a mental construct that is put down on paper, but rather an independent power, a kind of being that wants to be nourished. The more the vision is energized by everyone concerned, the stronger the impact of its pulling force will be, and the more comprehensively it will realize itself.

Antoine de Saint-Exupéry wrote: "…teach them to yearn for the vast and endless sea." In our particular case, the vision extended beyond the benefits for customers, employees, and entrepreneurs and also addressed the well-being of society. In comparison to our prior mission statement, we were now placing a greater emphasis on the company's service to the community. Our corporate vision was as follows:

- Music moves people and fosters a sense of community.
- Our company acts in the service of music.
- We are open to music of all styles and of all peoples and aim to create for it a bright, warm, and lively atmosphere.
- We enjoy a special bond with everyone for whom music is a profession or calling.
- Thanks to our vitality, innovative spirit, and enthusiasm, we are always at the pulse of what is happening in the world of music and on the music market.
- Our commitment, diligence, product range, and activities correspond to the needs of our customers and give rise to trust and lasting satisfaction.
- Our prices are in accord with the services we offer. They are fair, competitive, and credible.
- We are a workplace where individual talents are allowed to unfold through shared thoughts, feelings, and actions to the benefit of a meaningful whole.
- We are characterized by a positive basic attitude and therefore regard obstacles as opportunities.
- We assume responsibility for ourselves, our work, our company, and our environment.
- We cultivate a mutual "give and take" relationship with our business partners.
- We are an economically flourishing enterprise.
- Everything we do, we do as human beings for other human beings.

In contrast to a mission statement, a vision does not set goals but rather comprises the values and attributes necessary to implement them. We took care not to incorporate comparisons with other companies. The few clauses were intended to express personal accountability and to convey issues that were of importance to us in a clear and comprehensible manner. This meant that the vision could serve as an ever-present orientation aid that was accessible to everyone and that channeled the strengths of the entire workforce toward the common values. Regardless of the particular task within the company, everyone, in every situation, should be able to ask everyone else, "What about our values?" No one should be doing anything within the enterprise that conflicted with his personal convictions. Every staff member had the opportunity to voice his matters of concern for discussion. The corporate values that we had developed together formed a point of reference in this respect, with the result that we were always able to find solutions in accordance with these values.

A corporate structure that is exclusively hierarchical in nature can create neither a vision nor the freedom in which the vision can develop its pulling force. However, if we invoke an image on the horizon that is overflowing with joy, we create a fundamental wave within the enterprise that gives rise to appropriate actions in each individual situation. There is no better prerequisite for enabling employees to act in a personally accountable way than a deeply rooted and widely supported vision. When such a vision exists, the need for rules and regulations diminishes, because individuals find a meaningful purpose in contributing, through their work, toward realizing a model whose impact extends beyond the company itself and ultimately takes on global dimensions. There can be no greater motivational energy than that which arises when the corporate meaning is congruent with the meaning felt by the employee. This energy sustains everyone and guides the enterprise toward natural growth.

In practice, it is vital to continually rediscover what realizing a vision and its values entails. Each member of the company needs the ability and willingness, as well as the self-responsibility and inner freedom, to carefully and subtly integrate the vision into his area of work. A CD sales assistant who holds himself and his work in esteem will treat the customer with genuine friendliness. And as a rule, a customer who is served in such a manner will return. The friendly and competent charisma of a sales assistant has an appeal that is far greater than any artificially engendered advertising measure. Moreover, it is a gift that has an effect beyond the customer and the company. Something as minor as a smile on a shop assistant's face can have a major impact, just as each of our utterances influences the whole.

Naturally, there were also skeptics within the company who found it difficult to link these values with their specific work situations. After all, with the vision we were taking a leap into a future that we were describing as though it already existed. Some of our staff found this confusing. But despite initial opposition, in the end we were able to convince our critics that this tension between the "now" and the vision was essential if we were to move closer to realizing the vision. Without a clear perception of the present limitations, it is not possible to reduce them. After all, we only experience a particular situation as a limitation because the vision is already alive within us. Accordingly, this sometimes painful feeling is not the expression of deprivation, but rather of abundance, for the pain creates the very tension between the inside and the outside that ignites our creative potential for changing in the first place. Limitations and the ensuing feeling of being restricted trigger the contractions that give birth to something new—provided that we see the birth contractions in this light and refrain from paralyzing ourselves with judgments.

If we decide to fully accept the momentary situation, it will lead us into a process in which the vision can reveal itself in a more tangible manner—moving from the heart into matter.

As an entrepreneur, I have experienced how much more charisma and energy can be generated by a vision developed together with the employees than by mission statements that originate from within the higher echelons of a company. If the awareness process that this requires needs to be initiated and furthered by the company management, it is necessary for it to encompass the entire enterprise, from the bottom to the top; otherwise, it risks getting stuck halfway. Nowadays, I would involve not only the entire staff, but also representatives of the most important customers and suppliers, as well as spokespeople for those sectors of the public that are particularly affected by the company's operations.

Enterprises that are rooted in a spirit of service will openly declare their guiding values and respond competently to external and internal criticism, based on a naturally developed self-responsibility. They will also discover that no marketing or advertising measures can act as a substitute for the confidence in the company that is acquired in this way.

Community as a Corporate Culture

Martina: Is it possible, then, for a manager who does not want to change himself to develop and change his enterprise to the benefit of the community?

Hans: No, because a manager cannot instigate a community without wishing to become involved in it. There is a difference whether the manager derives his role from a hierarchical company structure or from the personal qualities that he wishes to make available to the employees. A person is a leader because he has something unique to contribute. If he draws his motivation from the depths of his inner being, he will not perceive the creative potential offered by a community as a threat to his own position, but instead will use it to its best advantage to change both himself and the company.

What does the word *community* actually mean to us? And why do we fear it just as much as we long for it? What do we expect from community, and where do we experience it? Why does it seem to be more natural to practice community in times of need than in everyday life?

Within a company, great importance is attached to teamwork, but to what extent is community actually allowed? Where does community begin and where does it end? Does a communal demonstration march already constitute an expression of community? And what purpose does community actually serve? Could it be that our yearning for community emanates from the deep-rooted knowledge of a field of collective wisdom from whose abundance we draw inspiration and that we wish to reproduce externally?

We probably all have the need to experience greater community, for example, in our personal relationships, within the family, or in the place where we live. However, our experience of interacting with each other does not always conform to our inner ideals and desires. So what distinguishes community? What are its attributes and where do our misconceptions lie?

If we trace the evolution of life and discern how increasingly complex organisms—organisms that are unable to exist without the individual characteristics of their various parts—developed out of a chaos of disordered energy, we have already identified one aspect of the essence of community. Community requires individuality; it nurtures the self-confidence and autonomy of its members. It differentiates and integrates at the same time.

The fear of self-abandonment is one misconception that is frequently associated with community. Anyone who has experienced the excessive demands of and misuse by so-called communities probably tends to view the concept of community with skepticism.

The members of a community, however, are not there to fill a supposed void in others in the way that, unfortunately, some parents expect from their children. Nor is it the purpose of a community to relieve individuals of their responsibility for their own actions. Instead, the members of a community respect the experiences and life concepts of the individual and *share* them with each another. In their view, communication is an exchange between equal partners.

Imagine for a moment our Western economy enjoying an equal partnership with those countries from whose resources it continually benefits! What is likely to change? What, indeed! And why should that which we accept—at least theoretically—as an equal partnership, such as marriage, for example, not also apply at the level of world economic trade?

In many companies, there is much talk about team strategy. But where is an enterprise that actively nurtures a community culture? Could it be that self-confidence on the part of the employees, which is inextricably linked with the concept of community, is only desired up to a certain point? What happens if, through finding their own self-value, employees also discover the value of the world around them? In the end, one does not exist without the other. Would the employees' self-image perhaps then extend beyond the market share that the company is continually striving for? Would they call into question existing organizational structures? And would this ultimately hurt or benefit the enterprise?

Instead of losing power, I gained confidence
in the wisdom of the community.

At our company, the latter was true. However, I can still clearly remember how frightened I was of losing my power when I agreed to hold the first vision sessions with our employees. It took a number of positive experiences before I gained confidence in the wisdom of the concept of community.

After thirty years of management experience, I had my first insight into the possibilities that community could offer through Robert, a young Chinese man who had been brought up in the Netherlands and who taught people how to consciously apply life energy by means of Taoist laws. The Chinese philosophy of Taoism (also known as Dao) teaches that reality, in all its diversity, emanates from a whole. Robert stayed with Elisabeth and me from time to time and taught us techniques, such as Qi Gong, that helped us to better perceive, strengthen, and implement our energy.

Convinced of the beneficial effect of these exercises, I asked Robert to hold courses for staff members who were interested in Qi Gong. As a result, the management team was already familiar with this energy work when we met with Robert for a weekend seminar.

One day during the seminar, Robert suddenly asked whether we were aware of a geometric shape in the room. As we were sitting in a circle, someone said that he could sense a circle touching our chests. We felt another such circle on our backs, at the same height as the first one. Both circles appeared to form a ring around us. Then an employee—someone from whom I would have least expected such a contribution—proposed that we place our new project in the middle of the circle. This project involved the renovation of some business premises to accommodate two large CD departments, a section for audio and video equipment, and an entire floor devoted to electronic musical instruments.

While we playfully took this project into our midst, each of us described it from his own perspective. One person predicted its impact on the market, another formulated the appeal it would have for the customers, someone else visualized the newly designed outlet, while the next one added elements that the others had overlooked.

In this manner, I experienced for the first time how useful it is to have a variety of viewpoints in order to discern the broad range of development possibilities offered by a given situation. I realized that the different perspectives of each individual could be collated to form a new, joint picture in which everyone can identify themselves. This gives rise to a consensus, by which everyone feels themselves to be borne.

We were able to base our subsequent corporate processes, including the vision work, on this experience. This superseded my predominantly hierarchical notion of corporate structures, which was ultimately based on the principle of "divide and rule." The old principle simply meant that the overview of all the corporate processes—and therefore also the power—was reserved for the management, while the individual employees were only granted insight into partial areas. Community needs leadership, but leadership without community lacks a deep-reaching impact. A manager who is not borne by a collective consensus is a lonely manager. The decisions of such a manager will not be carried by the rank and file in a personally accountable fashion and accordingly they quickly fade into nothingness. In such isolation, a leader can never feel entirely secure, and in turn this insecurity expresses itself in the form of protective mechanisms vis-à-vis the employees. One consequence of this is estrangement within the enterprise, which has a detrimental effect on the image of the company to the outside world.

To prevent this, many companies have started to rethink their procedures and are now implementing more team-oriented organizational structures. If these new structures evolve organically out of an internal change in values, the various levels of the enterprise will fit together to form an internal and external whole. However, if the new structures continue to serve merely as the means to an end, this will result more than ever in feelings of distrust between employees and management. Moreover, if the external form does not conform to the internal attitude, discrepancies in the management qualities will also become evident. Personal accountability and independence on the part of the employees will result in orders no longer being blindly obeyed. Consequently, a leader must take the time to find a consensus. Accordingly, community and leadership are not mutually exclusive; they are mutually dependent.

Therefore, anyone wishing to lead a group must be community-compatible and be ready time and time again to create community. It is true that the labor market, which previously comprised permanent positions, is increasingly being transformed into a project market where people are employed only on a temporary basis. But apart from the development of new forms of work and employment, in which effective cooperation is by no means any less in demand, hardly anyone knows how community actually evolves.

This very question brought me in contact with Scott Peck and his Foundation for Community Encouragement. Peck's community-building process lasts two days. In this course, a group of up to eighty participants attains the state of community, regardless of how heterogeneous the group is. I participated in a number of such processes, and on each occasion I was both astonished and moved to see how it is possible to reconcile so many life experiences and so many different opinions, ideas, and goals. By examining more closely the process that a group passes through in order to evolve into the state of community, it becomes clear how much our day-to-day experiences are reflected in such a process.

In his book *The Different Drum*, Peck refers to the individual maturity stages that a group goes through as pseudocommunity, chaos, emptiness, and, finally, community.

During the stage of pseudocommunity, the participants behave as if they are already a community, as if there are no disagreements between them. They are polite to one another, perhaps even too polite, for everyone is adhering to the unwritten rules that ostensibly characterize friendly, sociable people: Don't say anything that could offend someone else or is likely to provoke painful feelings. If someone does something that offends, annoys, or irritates you, don't let on, and change the subject as quickly as possible. Don't make yourself vulnerable or show your weaknesses. Keep your cool. Avoid showing your emotions and avoid conflict.

In pseudocommunity, none of the participants are authentic, which is one of the most important prerequisites for community. They withhold their emotions and keep their feelings to themselves.

If, however, a large number of people take part in a longer conversation, at some stage some of them are bound to say things that offend, annoy, or simply bore other members of the group. Michael might suddenly say, "People who get divorced should have thought more carefully about who they were marrying." Isabel, who is sitting three seats away and is currently in the throes of her third divorce, mumbles, half under her breath, "Yes, you're probably right," even though in reality she is furious at Michael's attitude.

One of the characteristics of pseudocommunity is that people tend to speak in generalities: "You always get the employees you deserve," "We should trust our intuition," "If you don't put profit first, you can't be a proper entrepreneur," "Abortion is a sin," or "Confident people are always successful." Because in pseudocommunity individual differences are denied and conflicts are avoided, such platitudes remain unchallenged. Pseudocommunity attempts to circumvent individual differences. But the more strongly these differences are repressed, the more strongly the pent-up energy leads the group into chaos.

In the chaos stage of community development, instead of sweeping the differences under the carpet, the participants elevate their own opinions to become the declared benchmark. Everyone tries to convert each other to their own views. The differences are now out in the open and considerable effort is spent obliterating them. However, the more the group attempts to reach a common denominator in this way, the more it drifts apart.

If a group does not move into the chaos stage on its own, the moderator might provide the necessary impetus. For example, the moderator might tell the participants that they are indulging in generalities and ask them to communicate with "I" statements in the future, whereupon George corrects his earlier statement and says, "For me, profit always takes top priority." "I'm glad you have now put it that way," replies John, "because I've discovered that I always come off best by putting my customers first." "We always need a mission," Eric accedes, which is yet another generalization, and then suddenly Irene counters that all this wishy-washy nonsense does not mean a thing to her. The period of politeness is over. Suddenly, everyone wants to impose their own views.

A typical expression of this state of chaos is always having solutions on hand to deal with other people's problems. "I have a problem balancing my work life with my family life," admits Irene. John immediately offers his advice: "If you take time every Sunday evening to make a plan for the entire week, you'll find it much easier to deal with this problem." "I've tried time management," replies Irene, "but it didn't help." "It's not a question of how much time we spend with the family," lectures Michael, "what's important is that it's quality time. When I realized this, my family problems vanished into thin air." "But I'm always so tired after work and feel really drained. There's no 'quality' in that," counters Irene, in an audibly dejected tone. "Why don't you attend a course on autogenous training," counsels George, without any pause for thought and with an utter lack of regard for the emotionality in Irene's last statement.

Neither differences nor painful feelings are allowed to exist. They are immediately covered up with helpful suggestions or comforting words. This stage of chaos often drags on tenaciously, even if it is completely clear to the group that it is right in the middle of it. The desire to "heal," to "convert," or to simply spontaneously express and force one's own views is just too great. What could be more logical in this stage than to attack the designated leader, to accuse him of poor leadership, and attempt to replace him? One such proposal might be: "This is getting us nowhere. Why don't we divide up into six small groups and first form a community there." Yet that would entail the very thing that hinders sustained community most—organization. In this stage of the community process, organization would merely serve to avoid the pain. Community develops by giving it space and allowing it to grow, not by structuring it.

If a group is prepared to experience chaos without relapsing into pseudocommunity, the process will then lead them to the next stage. Exhaustion from the battle of opinions, from the need to keep the situation under control (taking refuge with the doer), flows into emptiness. Avoidance tactics are no longer of any avail. The inner and outer chaos forces the individual into surrendering any previous control mechanisms. Now silence sets in.

This marks the turning point in the entire process, a shift from the need to try to force community to the willingness to accept the differences within the group, as well as one's own contradictions, without judging them. From the need to conform, participants shift to the courage to show one's self without a mask and to concede the same freedom to others. Earlier prejudices—such as "Just look at the clothes she's wearing!"—disappear, and now no one feels the need to convert or convince anyone else in order to avoid painful feelings. The group learns to bear the silence instead of seeking refuge in the noise of rapid responses as they did before. And finally the participants rid themselves of the restrictive expectations that they have, until now, associated with the notion of community. Nearly everyone who undergoes this community-building process has a preconceived idea of the form community should take. But genuine community will never exist as long as people refuse to empty their minds of preconceptions.

During the emptiness stage and the intensive listening that accompanies it, the first participants find the courage to voice very personal feelings, feelings that they need to rid themselves of in order to be fully present in the group and open themselves up to community. More often than not, suppressed disappointments and injured feelings come to light. For example, perhaps Eve tells about something that she experienced as a child, and Martin addresses a problem that directly concerns the group itself: "The way the such-and-such project was taken away from me three years ago still makes me angry even today."

Community requires authenticity and with it the courage to express painful feelings and allow oneself to be vulnerable. When the first members of the group find this courage, the others often react in an evasive fashion; they want to "heal" again and might even revert to chaos. In most cases, however, the group successfully makes the transition from emptiness to community.

Once the group has arrived at this point, the meaning of the following parable, which is recounted at the very beginning of each workshop by the process facilitator, suddenly becomes clear:

Once there was a monastic order whose spirit was in danger of drying up. The despondent abbot visited a rabbi in his woodland hermitage to seek his advice. The rabbi listened quietly and patiently to the abbot's story, but he had no advice to offer him. It was not until the abbot got ready to leave that, almost in passing, he said, "But the Messiah is among you."

Astonished, the abbot related the rabbi's words to the other monks. They looked at one another questioningly. Which of them could possibly be the Messiah? Brother X, who tends the plants with such loving care? Then again, he could sometimes be exceedingly obstinate. Or Brother Y, with his natural talent for dealing with animals—even though he did rather tend to eat too much? Thus each of them pondered on who the Messiah might be, and even secretly wondered if it could possibly be himself. As the monks contemplated each other's strengths and weaknesses, their perception of and esteem for both themselves and the others started to change. Soon they believed everyone in their community was capable of being the Messiah. And within a short period of time they became a thriving community once again.

If judgments transform themselves into compassion, isolation will turn into cooperation. With this new experience from the workshop under my belt, I devoted myself anew to the management of the company. I explained to my employees that I wanted to foster a culture of truthfulness and authenticity both within the company and with our customers, as well as in our advertising.

Initially, my idea met with restraint and distrust. But it was important to me that the employees took me at my word and did not silently carry out orders when they felt they would be betraying their values and convictions.

In my case, theory and practice were often worlds apart.

I was determined that this philosophy of truthfulness and authenticity should be applied even to seemingly trivial matters. For example, I no longer expected the receptionist to pretend that I was absent just because I did not wish to take phone calls. And if I nevertheless fell back into the old pattern of behavior, I wanted her to point this out to me.

In my mind's eye, I saw ourselves as the circle that we had sensed during the course with Robert, a circle that can only exist if each person is participating on an equal and authentic basis.

In my case, however, theory and practice were often worlds apart. However, now I noticed the discrepancy myself. I thus learned that community always also entails working with one's own unconscious shadow.

On one occasion, I became very annoyed when an employee from our advertising agency presented us with a draft of our customer card that I did not like. The "crime" he had committed was nothing more than the fact that no empty space had been left to add the customer's name. Our discussion proceeded something along these lines: "I've already explained this three times, but I'll explain it to you a fourth time too…" My counterpart, however, was not prepared to put up with this tone. "In that case," he retorted, "I would be grateful if you would finally provide me with a complete concept of what you want." Unprepared for this reproach, I shouted at the staff member sitting beside me, who was responsible for the project, "I told you on the phone that the concept must state that the sales staff should address the customer by name." "I'd forgotten to include that," she admitted somewhat remorsefully. The advertising consultant chipped in again, "But your sales personnel don't address customers by name anyway, even when they see it on their credit card." Irritated, I replied that this was no reason for not doing what I wanted. It was clear that we were not going to reach a consensus. Due to my impatience and my self-opinionated attitude, I had stifled all creativity. The meeting resulted in nothing more than false expectations, accusations, and defensive reactions that were of no use to anyone. Instead of forming a collective circle and viewing the matter to be decided on from this perspective, each person felt that his own opinion was being threatened and thus formed his own circle with himself in the middle. According to Scott Peck, this is a typical example of the chaos stage in the community development process. No wonder I felt awful after the meeting. A week later, the advertising consultant and I sat together once more and quickly reached an agreement. This time, the discussion was relaxed. We decided to leave a line in the block-letter grid free and to add an explanatory remark for the customer: "If we may address you by your name, please enter it here." The solution was as simple as that.

In such cases, I was not—and still am not—left with any choice other than to accept myself, complete with my limitations. Consequently, I also ought to accept limitations in others. Real communication, collective movement, and change all arise solely out of compassion for ourselves and for others.

However, this unfoldment of consciousness within our company required both practice and patience. After all, the working relationship that had previously been based on giving instructions and exerting control could not be transformed overnight into collaboration and personal accountability. But we had created the foundation for our corporate structure to change from its hitherto hierarchical setup into an arrangement of interconnecting circles. Like the various organs in the body, each department in the company also had its own specific function.

The smaller circles, or organisms, each work as a team, while the team leaders converge to form a larger, encompassing circle, so that an interconnected "holarchic" structure emerged. (See graphic next page)

Because the team leaders at all the levels felt themselves to be part of a larger community, their spirit in turn reached the smaller units, or circles, and vice versa. Thus, an interdependency arose within the corporate organism that invariably had an impact on the whole.

This in effect marked the start of the transformation process of the company and led shortly afterward to our collective vision work. The experience of this community also helped me when I had to break the news to the twenty-two employees of Musica AG, a wholesale firm founded twenty-five years earlier, that we would be forced to close down the company due to the evidently irreversible development of the market.

I called all the employees affected by this closure together into a circle to inform them of our decision in good time. After I had delivered the bad news, everyone seemed to be in a state of shock. One of the employees suggested that it might be better to meet again the following day, to give everyone time to digest what they had just been told. When we gathered again in the circle the next morning, all of the employees' anger and aggression was directed at me. I knew that I would have to confront their wrath if I wanted everyone to regain their strength. In the weeks that followed, we continued these rounds and gradually an intensive exchange developed between the employees. During these sessions, they discussed their particular situations and encouraged each other to regard this crisis as an opportunity. One person decided to go into business on his own and told the group, "I'm still looking for two people." Another admitted he had been waiting for this moment to start something new. The exchange within the circle had a healing effect on everyone. We found it much easier to come to terms with the initial feelings of despair this way than if we had attempted to do so by means of individual discussions. On their last workday, all employees except one had found a new job.

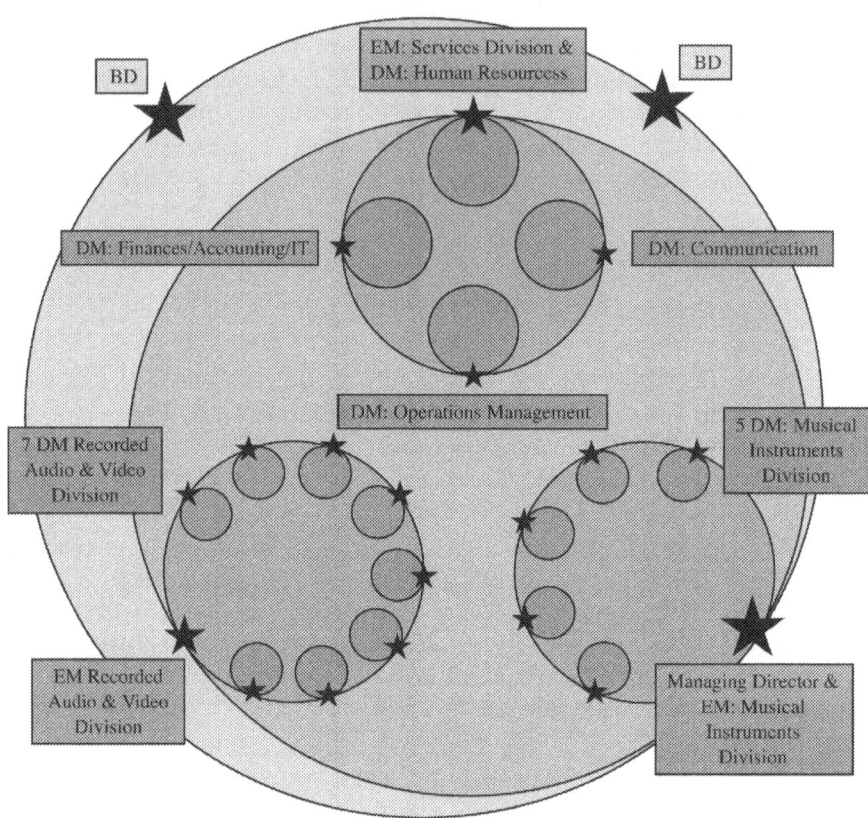

Holorganigram of Jecklin & Co. AG, 1998

The fields marked in increasingly dark shades show the various corporate levels: BD (Board of Directors), EM (Executive/Division Management) and DM (Department Management). Each wider reaching level incorporates all of the levels contained within it. Each department manager (DM) is on the one hand the leader of the team of employees in his individual department, and on the other, a member of the team responsible for his particular division (Services, Musical Instruments, Recorded Audio & Video). The executive managers (EM) are simultaneously leaders of the team of department managers for their particular division and members of the Executive Management team. The leader of the executive managers is, as Managing Director, also a member of the team serving on the Board of Directors.

A key element that makes it possible to move on from pseudocommunity is without doubt the courage to be authentic, coupled with a growing ability to acknowledge individual viewpoints as aspects of the whole. In order to practice this more, we introduced the "we round" with which I had become acquainted during my stay in the slum of Ibayo. This manner of sharing helps the members of a group to shed their individual ballast. Therefore, I asked the employees to engage in this exchange, naturally on a voluntary basis.

We held these "we rounds" before our senior management meetings in order to create the prerequisite for opening ourselves up to what other people had to say and to become attuned to the group's field of collective wisdom. Such a round would begin with each participant describing his present state of mind as an individual. This might comprise completely mundane statements, such as "I'm tired today," or "I'm on edge because I'm sad," or simply "I'm angry." The response to the next question, "How do I feel as part of the company?" might be, "I don't feel that I'm being appreciated enough," or "I'm having problems applying my convictions in my work." The third and last question, "How do I feel as a world citizen?" was particularly difficult for the participants to answer. Often they found that they were so caught up with themselves that they were overwhelmed by this question.

But as soon as we discussed the purpose of our activities not just vis-à-vis our employees and customers but also in relation to the needs of the entire planet, this question opened the way for us to progress from the needs of the individual to those of the whole. Sometimes, however, the third question led to a general feeling of resignation. Faced with the conflicts taking place all over the world, a feeling of helplessness spread among us. If I sensed this underlying trend at the end of a "we round," I would relate to the group, among other things, what I had learned from an "enlightened" management consultant. His advice was to consciously deal with the daily horror reports in the media by analyzing them in relation to what they had to do with oneself. A news item that moves us emotionally begs the question as to whether we feel called upon and have the means to provide assistance and actively make a difference. If so, we should follow the call and act; if not, it means that our own inner wounds have been accosted by the external events and we need to attend to them. Merely lamenting the state of the world without reflecting on one's own position is both pointless and unproductive.

Apart from the fact that I occasionally addressed the general mood of those present before concluding the sharing session, one basic rule of this "we round" was not to respond to someone who had just spoken. Everyone should be able to speak openly about their concerns, without the group attempting to convert, comfort, or evaluate the speaker. In this manner, we listened to one another, learned to take in the various experiences, and refrained from trying to change someone else's point of view. Nothing was considered to be wrong; everything was permitted. This freedom allowed an ensuing business meeting to acquire the openness and vitality that are conducive to making meaningful decisions.

Nonetheless, during a rather stressful phase of our activities, I neglected this community-building tool. Once again I considered it necessary to act in accordance with the maxim "Time is money." This continued until the personnel manager approached me on her own accord and asked that we reintroduce the "we rounds." "Then our meetings proceed in a completely different manner," she said. "You, too, are more open than when you simply plunge headlong into a problem." I was grateful for this feedback, especially because this time the impetus for increased community had come from the employees themselves. Quite apart from the fact that time cannot be measured in terms of money or vice versa, I am convinced that every investment in community ultimately recoups itself through the effectiveness of the results.

As a group, we alternated between pseudocommunity and chaos and, if things went well, we also achieved emptiness and even the occasional experiences of community. It was possible to spot which stage of communication prevailed at any given time, not only within the individual departments, but also within a conflict. One example of this concerned the dismissal of a staff member.

"That X again!" I thought when it was discovered that a payment to one of our suppliers had been overlooked and word came from the bookkeeping department that Mr. X was responsible. The reason for my reaction was that this was not the first time such a slipup had occurred. On my return to the operational management of the company after a lengthy absence, I had come across a fax from a Spanish recording engineer, who informed us that instead of the agreed sum of 70,000 pesetas, our company had in fact transferred to his account the same sum in Swiss francs. While he could certainly put this money to very good use, he did not feel comfortable about the situation and was anxious to reimburse the excess sum.

As things had not been limited to just this one mistake, I decided to dismiss Mr. X. I voiced my intention at the next senior management meeting. While Mr. X's direct superior agreed in principle, he did not think it was fair to base the dismissal on the mistakes that had been made prior to this last mishap. Without responding to this objection, I once again listed off all the recent irregularities, insisted on a dismissal, and went off on holiday. During my absence, our personnel manager conducted the dismissal talks with Mr. X. He rejected the accusations and insisted on talking directly with me. On my return to the office, I was unable to deny his request. With my gaze riveted to the desk, I began the conversation with, "Mr. X, you are continually making mistakes," and I then proceeded to spell them all out. He replied that I could not prove without a shadow of doubt that he had made these mistakes; it might just as easily have been someone else. Our conversation did not proceed well. I sensed how unhappy he was and was suddenly aware of how uncertain I was about whether this dismissal was really justified after all.

The next morning, I brought up my feelings of discomfort at the senior management meeting. "I think that we all agree that Mr. X does not fit in here," I said. "The situation is no longer acceptable, neither for him nor for us." Everyone expressed their agreement. However, I had to admit that I would have much rather preferred to have had some airtight reasons for his dismissal. I found it considerably easier to cling to Mr. X's mistakes than to address our unsatisfactory collaboration over the previous months.

The difficulties had begun when we had been forced to close down Musica AG. Prior to the closure, Mr. X had been responsible for the central accounting at this company. We knew that he had just bought a house and that both of his daughters were still at school. Unemployment was rising in Switzerland, and under these circumstances a dismissal would have hit him hard. Therefore we thought that we were helping him when, following the closure of Musica AG, he was transferred to the department at Jecklin that handled accounts payable and payment transactions. However, this new area of work entailed a downgrade in his responsibilities; after all, at Musica AG he had been in charge of the central accounting. All of a sudden, this somewhat conservative man in his fifties found himself working in a team of young people, which made him feel like an outsider. Instead of putting a time limit on our thoughtful gesture, which at the time had seemed to make sense, a "temporary permanent" solution had arisen that neither party was happy about but also did not feel able to openly address.

With this foremost in my mind, I had another talk with Mr. X. In the previous discussion, he had reproached me for the fact that, instead of making him senior accountant of the entire company, we had hired someone younger to take on the task. He now asked me again for the true reasons for his dismissal, and this time I was able to clearly tell him.

Now that I had freed the conversation of my original accusations and brought up the actual problem of our collaboration, Mr. X was relieved. "I can go along with that," he told me. "This is helpful. When you talk to me on this level I'm grateful for your initiative. I've felt all of these things, too, but never had the courage to make the first move. Now I'm glad that you are sending me off to look for something new."

From pseudocommunity—the mutual acceptance of an unacceptable situation—via the chaos of reciprocal accusations, we had found truthfulness, without which we would never have been able to reach a consensus.

I was able to assuage Mr. X's initial concern that at his age he would have little chance of finding a job by offering to support him by furthering his skills and financing training courses for him.

The atmosphere was now relaxed. The key had been to cease placing the blame on the employee. Thanks to this episode, I discovered that it required much more courage for me to openly admit that I felt that we were not on the same wavelength than it did to accuse him of making mistakes. As soon as my own feelings came into play, I found myself venturing into unknown territory.

Authenticity begins with perceiving
one's own state of mind, emotions, and prejudices.

Yet it is exactly at the point where authenticity begins that community becomes possible in the first place. Addressing our own state of mind means assuming responsibility for our feelings, instead of proceeding to the level of accusations and assignment of guilt in order to avoid exposing ourselves to our inner limitations. My experience with Mr. X confirmed how important it is for the future of both parties that they talk to each other, before going their separate ways, to rid themselves of anything that was encumbering the employment relationship and could, if it remained unresolved, continue to have a detrimental effect on the person's next job. In our experience, processes that lead to the termination of a working relationship in mutual esteem are always fruitful for both sides; the employee is given the opportunity to find a new job for which he or she is better suited—which was ultimately the case with Mr. X—and the company is able to take on someone who is more suitable for the position.

From then on, I upheld the rule that I should enter into an exchange with an employee who failed to comply with a mutual agreement. On doing so, it was always clear in my mind that inadequacy at the workplace does not signify inadequacy as a human being, but rather that the person's talents and the requirements of the job are incompatible.

In this regard, we have also parted ways with managers who were incapable of leadership. Professional competence does not necessarily go hand in hand with the ability to confront conflicts in a constructive way. There were managers who, for fear of losing themselves in chaos, with all its contradictions and friction, clung to the pseudocommunity of their team. Conflicts were simply ignored. And if they did become evident, they were swiftly eradicated, usually by means of pressure.

In one such case, a manager spoke to each of his departmental heads individually and asked them to think about possible shortcomings within their sphere of responsibility. "You must think about why your department is doing so badly. The boss wants to know my opinion by Friday, which means that I have to know by Thursday what I should tell him." Yet what was important to me was the collective process both within the departments themselves and within the team of departmental heads. Conflicts that cropped up within these levels should also be collectively considered and dealt with at their respective level. In these processes, a leader would act, so to speak, as a coach. If he was unable to deal with a conflict because it triggered his own unconscious fears, the leader would fight his inner threat in the outside world by means of pressure, thereby paralyzing the entire team.

Here, too, it was plain to see that teamwork involves confronting one's own shadow. Honest communication requires that we work on our inner transformation. A leader, in particular, must be willing to do this, for without the ability to accept internal and external conflicts, to embrace them as creative potential and also deal with them in this spirit, the individual will not grow in strength, nor will a group develop into a community.

In contrast to the industrial age, in which only measurable results counted ("time is money"), the information age is totally geared toward communication, that is, the conscious integration of internal processes into an external form of expression. The definition of what we understand by the word "work" also changes in this respect. Its interpretation departs from the increasingly narrow paths of objective facts and expands into the area of inner and initially invisible consciousness work. Until now, this type of integrative creativity has principally been attributed to artists. Their creative work presupposes authenticity and personal accountability. In the future, authenticity and personal accountability will be indispensable for all of us, with respect to both the individual and the collective consciousness evolution, as well as with a view to the working worlds that are changing as a result.

We would be mistaken to believe that developed communities are free of conflicts. Rather, they know how to deal with conflicts in a personally accountable fashion. Each member of the community can potentially also be a leader. Personal accountability within a community results in the individual being able, through individual talents, to take on responsibility within the group, depending on which qualities are required at that particular time. Individuals will be motivated to do so not by a disproportionate craving for recognition, but by the natural desire to share their talents with others. Personal accountability presupposes that the individual's self-esteem is not dependent on acknowledgment from the outside. Once people have developed an awareness of their own strengths and abilities, they wish to share their talents. What else should they do, if not use their abilities for the common good? People who assume responsibility for themselves by having a high level of self-regard are also able to assume responsibility for the community. They will not try to dominate others in order to build up their self-confidence. Instead, they regard themselves as trustees of the community, to whose essence they are true—and are thereby also true to themselves.

Women seem to have a greater understanding than men when it comes to linking responsibility for oneself with that for the community. At least, this is evident in the example of the Grameen Bank, which was first set up in Bangladesh and is regarded in many places as a model for granting very small loans. These "microcredits" are awarded by small committees of women who know the borrowers personally. In India, I became acquainted with women's handicraft cooperatives that took advantage of such tiny loans to finance the tools and raw materials that they required. In their model, 10 percent of the turnover is channeled into marketing activities carried out by the small-scale entrepreneurs, 30 percent is invested in communal infrastructures, and 60 percent of the revenue flows back to the entrepreneurs themselves. This portion is also used to repay the loans. The women know that if the loans are not repaid, there will be no funds for future projects. Furthermore, they feel accountable to the committee that granted them the loans in the first place. Experiences with granting such microcredits to men were negative in comparison to the repayment rates of the women. In such cases, everyone looked after their own interests first. This may be due to the broken self-confidence of many of the men in formerly colonized countries. Personal accountability, and therefore responsibility for the community, invariably go hand in hand with a well-developed sense of self-esteem. A person who wishes to impress others as a doer has not yet recognized himself or herself as being an equal part of a community.

In this regard, leadership means the very opposite of being a doer. It implies getting involved in and sharing with the community instead of disassociating oneself from it. In a well-developed community, no one comes off badly. Such a community encourages individuals to lead so that everyone can benefit from their talents. In a developed community, leadership is not confused with the status symbol of a doer, before whom the group must bow down so that the leader feels tall. Instead, leadership within the context of a developed community means ensuring an even balance of the energy that flows through the group, nothing more and nothing less. In a community, the natural flow of give and receive is practiced.

Moving on from unproductive pseudocommunity and experiencing equal cooperation frees a person of role assignments and expectations that no one can continually live up to anyway. The assumption of a position of leadership is not always perceived as a privilege, not only because the pressure to succeed grows, but also because the distance to the employees increases. It can be very cold and lonely at the top. As long as companies stress the difference between those at the top and those "down below," careers may perhaps be guaranteed, but the health and well-being of both those affected and the company itself suffer as a result.

Referring back to Peck's community-building process, the stages that lead to forming a community are similar to the stages of transformation that a person undergoes in a personal crisis. Upon closer examination, the dialogues of the players that we portrayed earlier are by the same token also alive within us; the disavowal of circumstances as they manifest themselves externally corresponds to the repression and rejection of the related consciousness powers within us—the thoughts, emotions, and even bodily reactions (Peck's pseudocommunity stage). And if this repression does not function on an ongoing basis, anger at the situation, and with it the chaos within us, erupt (Peck's chaos stage). As soon as we are sufficiently exhausted by the anger, there is room for sadness and silence or for experiencing the "now" (Scott Peck's emptiness stage). This in turn leads to acknowledgment and acceptance of the present situation, and therefore to the synergy of the strengths within us that had previously been thrown off balance (Peck's community stage). Each time we undergo chaos and our inner strengths subsequently find a new order, we transform ourselves and are renewed. As goes the inside, so goes the outside.

After successfully building a community, we may mistake the group that acted as catalyst when we experienced the creative abundance of transformation for the abundance itself, with the result that we become dependent on the group. Abundance, however, is not dependent on people and external circumstances but is within us. Autonomy and community are mutually dependent on each other. Community in this sense cannot create dependency. Community becomes a constructive force only if it is based on the interaction of personally accountable individuals. It does not provide a place to hide. Instead, it forces us into continual self-actualization, for our dark side reveals itself primarily when we are in conflict with others.

I experienced this in the Swiss army at the tender age of twenty-one. As a newly qualified officer, I was in charge of a platoon of approximately thirty soldiers, most of whom were almost twice my age. The final exercise of our refresher course involved crossing a river and a forest at night. This meant we had to be as quiet and invisible as possible, which ruled out torches, smoking, and conversation. In addition to personal baggage and a weapon, each soldier had to carry more than twenty-five kilograms of additional weapon parts or ammunition. As an officer, I was exempted from having to lug around this extra load.

After some time, I heard the first muted cries from the rear of the platoon. "Aren't we going to have any breaks?" I thought to myself, "Yes, I suppose that would be okay," and announced in a whisper, "Put down your loads and fall out." Naturally the men pulled out their cigarettes, but I turned a blind eye so as not to deprive them of this small pleasure. After a quarter of an hour, I felt that the break had been long enough. I remembered the commands that I had learned and ordered, "Jecklin platoon up!" Nothing happened. It was vital to keep noise to an absolute minimum, so I hissed once again, "Up!" Muffled giggling filtered out from the darkness. I repeated the command with helplessly authoritative insistence. "This is an order! Get up and pick up your loads!" This time there was outright laughter. What should I do? I took a different tack. "Look, we're all part of this exercise; we've got to get out of this forest together sometime." "That's easy for you to say. You don't have to carry anything," retorted a soldier. Another of the men moaned that he could scarcely walk another step and his whole body ached under his load. Indeed, I had nothing to carry except my pistol, so I relieved him of his load. When I then ordered the group to proceed, there were no longer any objections.

An officer's stripe on his uniform may be impressive during the day. But in the dark, its impact is lost. Then, only authenticity and credibility count.

Corporate Management
and Inner Guidance

Martina: How would you describe inner guidance?

Hans: In my view, it is inherent wisdom that reaches far beyond our own personal perspectives. I also call it my "inner self," my true being. Surrendering to this inner self also requires opening oneself up to a broad spectrum of unanticipated possibilities.

Martina: In other words, if I allow myself to be led by my inner self, I can make decisions that take into account not only a partial aspect of a problem, but the problem—with all its interrelated aspects—as a whole.

Hans: Yes, our inner self motivates each of us to integrate, so to speak. Being spiritual does not in any way mean escaping from the world, as is often implied. Rather, our spirituality enables us to behave in a constructive manner, to recognize the diversity and interconnections of the world, and to feel at one with it.

Martina: This means that intuition is like an ambassador of the inner self. It provides the answer, derived from the very core, to a given situation.

At some time or another, we have all experienced something suddenly dawn-ing on us out of the blue. Perhaps it is an idea or a solution to a problem with which we have been grappling for some time. More often than not, this type of intuitive impulse also signals that a change in behavior is long overdue. We receive the message but find it difficult to rely on, as it does not fit into our belief system. The fears and reservations that cause us to ignore the message— consciously or unconsciously—are for the most part so powerful that we avoid making a change, preferring to adhere to our old behavioral patterns.

Moreover, we are not always certain if we are perceiving an intuitive message or simply reacting to a mechanism with which we are sabotaging ourselves. Inner voices can be multifaceted. Fears, desires, and beliefs can get in the way, and these emotions are often difficult to distinguish from inner guidance. As we become more receptive to our own spirituality, the unresolved fears or shadows residing in our unconscious start to make themselves heard and trig-ger our emotions.

For this reason, I try not to make any decisions if I feel I am caught up in my underlying emotions. When I am consumed by anger or pain, I can be certain that these emotions have less to do with a particular external stimulus and more to do with inner fears that have been evoked by the given scenario. Only when I am able to carefully observe what is taking place within myself emo-tionally do I have the distance not to be caught off guard. It is therefore help-ful to differentiate between these inner voices when making decisions, in order to avoid creating situations that have been shaped by hidden fears. This is eas-ier said than done, since it is hard to distinguish which voice is saying what. It requires practice to clear out the clutter and to distance oneself from an inci-dent and the accompanying emotions and thought patterns.

In this respect, I have found meditation to be a very useful practice. Through meditation, I have been able to attain a sense of serenity, security, and tran-quility, which now helps me discern whether a message is stemming from my inner guidance or from my fears and beliefs.

However, the increasing ability to discern and recognize the inner voices has another side to it. A friend of mine once said to me, "You are becoming more sensitive, and that has a great advantage: you are becoming more sensitive. But there is also a great disadvantage: you are becoming more sensitive."

Meditation leads to heightened sensitivity, and this indeed has two facets. By becoming more aware of our true selves, we feel happier, more confident, and at greater peace with the world. At the same time, this process requires work, because our shadows, too, suddenly become adamant about being noticed.

This is not surprising, as usually from an early age we practice repressing our emotional wounds, which from then on fester in the form of unconscious fears. They subsequently influence our thoughts, our feelings, and even our physical being. Just when it appears as though the air has cleared, these repressed feelings bubble to the surface again. They are no longer concerned about being stifled. In a sense, fears can be considered our housemates. If we try to shut them out, they will most certainly come in through the back door. They will continue to create havoc until we muster up the courage to consciously invite them inside. Inner growth entails developing this courage.

Ironically, practicing meditation and inner growth is misunderstood by both skeptics and fervent devotees alike as a way to escape external challenges. In fact, it is just the opposite; the more I trust my inner guidance, the more I am in the position and ready to examine my inner shadows in depth. I do not have to project them onto the outside world. In fact, I will not be able to do anything other than develop into an accountable and self-confident person, and this will have an effect on my ability to have relationships, on my profession, and on my relationship with the world as a whole.

Meditation makes you thin-skinned—
and the conflict with your own shadows
is not long in coming.

It goes without saying that such a development cannot take place without some friction. Initially, perhaps, we even tax the patience of those around us with our more intense emotions and narrow-minded way of thinking. I have been meditating on a regular basis for many years, but I can still clearly remember when I started. After my morning meditation, I would go to my office feeling well-balanced and friendly. The first irritation would barely upset me. One incantation that I repeated to myself like a mantra was "I am peaceful." This would continue to have an effect even when a second disturbance arose. However, if a third problem suddenly materialized, I would explode. The person who triggered this unintentional explosion was subjected to such a browbeating that it took his or her breath away. To top it off, if anyone came up with the brilliant idea of asking if it was true that I meditated, the day was over as far as I was concerned.

Most people imagine that someone who meditates is automatically easygoing and friendly. Therefore, it comes rather as a surprise that meditation also makes a person more thin-skinned and, in fact, can cause their shadows to become more noticeable. While I became sensitive, I was not very good at dealing with it. Today, I know how important it is to supplement this sensitization that is accompanied by tranquility with work on one's own shadow and to also seek the support of a friend, therapist, or teacher who has experience in such issues. If I start to observe my surroundings more intensely, I also must learn to cope with the consequences of this heightened perception. External circumstances can activate inner shadows, but instead of blaming the outside world, it is essential to find out what is rebelling and causing pain on the inside.

In Japan, it is not unusual for firms to finance Zen monasteries, where their employees regularly participate in meditation courses. By providing these courses, companies hope to make their staff work more effectively. Apparently, though, the companies are not primarily concerned with spiritual growth. But as the Zen master of one of the monasteries laughingly explained, "However, without even wanting it, something altogether quite different takes place, and that is why we agree to the deal."

Meditation is a way to develop consciousness. As a patiently practiced exercise, it takes us into the depths of our very being, where separation between consciousness and form, subject and object, internal and external no longer exists. For those who have had this experience, nothing will be as it was before. Such an experience will radically question any behavior that is based on the "divide and rule" principle. Here is precisely where the hopes of the Zen master lie when he says he is glad to have the meditating managers in his monastery. Consistent meditation, and the subsequent changes and responsibilities that occur as a result, will give rise to a wiser and gentler way of interacting with the world.

We have grown accustomed to separating the internal from the external. However, from the perspective of inner guidance, there is only one all-encompassing consciousness, which expresses itself in its diversity. Certainly one reward of meditation is the fact that practitioners begin to grasp and comprehend complex problems in their deeper, interconnected relationships. From this integrated perspective, life phases and experiences form a leitmotif, even if up to that point they do not appear to be connected. However, as is stated in the film *A River Runs Through It*, "Eventually, all things merge into one, and a river runs through it." This "eventually" begins by making conscious contact with our inner guidance.

I have often only understood the signs of my inner guidance in hindsight, such as when I think back to our unexpected commercial success with Maxell cassettes. We all have our own stories about how we became acquainted with our inner guidance. These stories tell of both joyful and painful experiences. If we begin in this way to accept everything that we encounter as a learning process, we are led toward becoming who we really are.

In retrospect, I realize that, time and again, at decisive moments in my life I have encountered people and generated events that have helped me on my journey along this path. The trip to Ganeshpuri and my new training in a completely different sphere are among the key spiritual stimuli that have had a lasting effect on everything that subsequently wanted to develop, both internally and externally.

Elisabeth and I went to visit our friends Bernhard and Rashna Imhasly in India. During our stay, Rashna introduced Elisabeth to Chris Griscom's book *Time Is an Illusion*, in which the eminent American reincarnation therapist describes the experiences and successes of her therapy. Elisabeth was enthusiastic about this work relating to past life regression. She immediately made an appointment at Chris Griscom's Light Institute in New Mexico and started making her travel arrangements. At first, I was unable to share her enthusiasm. Past lives had never really interested me. But Elisabeth could not be deterred, and as I had business to attend to in Los Angeles anyway, we flew together to the United States. We parted in Los Angeles and arranged to meet later in Chicago at a trade fair. When I arrived at the hotel at the appointed time and searched for our room down the winding corridors of the old Hilton Hotel, I heard from afar Elisabeth's laugh as she struggled with the magnetic lock on the door. The laugh sounded as if it were coming from a transformed Elisabeth. It won me over instantly, and a few months later I, too, was on my way to the Light Institute.

During the past-lives sessions I attended there, a different world opened up to me, and I began to trust in the meaning of my life in a completely new way. A powerful inner experience enabled me to understand at once what made my life important, independent from outer appearances.

I experienced how I was violently pushed off a rock cliff. My body plunged into the depths. However, contrary to the mortal agony that is suggested in action thrillers, something completely different happened to me. During the freefall, I became a knowing observer. I watched my body hit the ground as lifeless matter. Evidently this body was dead. Yet I was still alive. And while all this was happening, I did not have the impression that there was anything strange about it! However, following the session I was overwhelmed by what I had experienced—and at the same time extremely relieved. For the first time in my life, I experienced myself as a spiritual being, which indeed *had* a body, but was not the body. How could this be possible? Something that I called "I" appeared to be fully awake, lucid, and able to perceive what had happened, while my physical body lay lifeless on the ground. What was this entity that existed independently of my body?

Barbara Gluck, one of Chris Griscom's coworkers, who was later to become my teacher, helped me to better understand my experience. Her interpretation is consistent with the experiences of many people who have gained insight into the spectrum of their consciousness through past-life sessions, spiritual training, a near-death encounter, or some other form of transpersonal experience. Reports of such experiences appear in the lore of different epochs and cultures, and they conjoin with the spiritual philosophy of our time. According to these experiences, the soul is an invisible fabric. It is described as a spiritual core—the inner self—surrounded by mental, emotional, and ethereal layers of consciousness. These different layers penetrate our physical bodies as long as we live. In death, they appear to separate from the body.

This is exactly what I experienced during my past-life therapy. And because this subtle fabric contains its own memory in which our life experiences are stored, I did not perceive the shift from having a body to being bodiless as a great loss. After all, I took with me my consciousness—the mental sphere with all the thoughts and visions I had been holding in my mind throughout my life; the emotional part where all my feelings, with all their fluctuations and wounds, are stored; and my ethereal body, the cell memory of the physical body, which carries within it the oldest and most traumatic experiences.

Above all, the journey into the world of my soul revealed the core of its hidden being—my inner self, which with its universal awareness and love reminded me that in my true being I am undamaged, whole, and eternal.

When we enter the cycle of life—or rather the cycle of experiences in the dual world governed by the forces of attraction and repulsion—we lose our awareness of being one with our source and fall prey to the illusion of being separated from it; hence our entanglement in the materialistic manifestation of the soul. As we no longer feel complete, we seek compensation in outer security. This is another illusion, which leads us even further into outer dependence. However, this illusion, essentially connected with all the human traumas and experiences, is precisely our chance, because as there is nothing beyond this one spirit, the illusion is also just another one of its games; it leads the doer down a dead-end street, which again and again provides the opportunity to recognize and awaken to the inner self.

We can also discover subtle bodies or fields of the soul in corporations. It was interesting for me as a businessman to try to understand the soul of a company and its influence on all the people working there. Based on this insight, together with our employees, we discovered the common corporate vision of our company. It is always the inner knowledge, the potential of the community, that mutually attracts and unites individual employees. This convergence does not happen by coincidence. The collective consciousness field possesses its own affinity to realize itself.

During the past-life sessions at the Light Institute, I began to understand these interrelationships. I also heard that Chris Griscom was planning to be in India at the same time as us and that she was urgently looking for partners who would be interested in organizing seminars for her. Naturally our friends Bernhard and Rashna in New Delhi immediately sprang to mind.

Thus the circle, which had begun with the book tip from Rashna, closed, and all of us—Barbara Gluck, Chris Griscom and her children, and Elisabeth and I—met at the Imhaslys' in India. After Chris's seminars were finished, Rashna proposed that we all go to visit the ashram of Swami Gurumayi Chidvilasananda in Ganeshpuri, a spiritual center to which Rashna had felt closely bonded since her youth. Without hesitation, we all agreed to go along. Elisabeth and I had always secretly imagined meeting a spiritual teacher during one of our trips to India. Nevertheless, we were skeptical. Standing in front of the gate to the ashram, we promised each other never to become dependent on a guru.

The ashram appeared more beautiful to us than any other park we had visit-ed in India. As we entered, with the sun streaming down on us, we saw Gurumayi—whose master Swami Muktananda had founded the ashram—sitting in an elevated position in the center of a huge courtyard. A large num-ber of people were grouped around her, with men and women seated apart. We looked for a spot toward the back to observe everything from a safe dis-tance. Apparently Gurumayi had just returned from a pilgrimage with some of her devotees. An account of the trip was delivered by an extremely articu-late master of ceremonies in the style of an American talk show host, which had a sobering effect on us. Nonetheless, when after an hour we caught each other's eye, we found that they were full of tears. Without being able to put our finger on what it was, something we had experienced there had touched us profoundly.

On the following day, we participated in a *darshan*, a type of encounter with a teacher, commonly found in Hinduism, in which one's own inner self is touched by that of the teacher. A long queue had formed. Those who arrived in front of Gurumayi bent down, touched the ground with their foreheads, and were given a blessing with a frond of ostrich feathers. Luckily our friends had explained the meaning of the ceremony to us beforehand. The bowing is not directed at the teacher as a person, but rather at the presence of his eternal self, which flows so strongly through the teacher that one's own inner self can be touched and sensed. The ritual did not serve to worship the guru, but to become aware of the master within ourselves. I was glad to have received this cultural tutoring from my friends. Without their input, we would have had dif-ficulty embracing this experience.

On the way back to the place where I had been sitting, I heard Gurumayi call out the name Hans. I found it amusing that evidently someone else was pres-ent who shared my name. It did not occur to me that *I* could be the one she was referring to. But a few men pointed to me, so I made my way to the front again. I saw Elisabeth already sitting on the ground next to Gurumayi. She pointed me toward a stone step close to where she was seated and then focused her attention again on the darshan.

About an hour later, the crowd had subsided, but people stayed to meditate or simply sit quietly on the ground in the courtyard. I had not noticed that Gurumayi had stood up. I was only aware of a shadow, and then I felt her hand on my head. At that moment, I was flooded with a stream of light so intense that I was blinded by its luminosity, and for at least one minute I could not see.

After this incident, my mind was in turmoil. What I had felt at the touch of Gurumayi's hand confirmed the reality of my experience during my past-life sessions. I also became physically aware that I was an element of a force much greater than myself. Every day and every night I spent at the ashram drew me deeper into this force. I lay awake at night, enveloped by an indescribable feeling of joy that poured out of my heart.

The deep awareness of our own selves
ultimately leads us to experiencing our inner wisdom.

We had this first encounter with Gurumayi in 1988. After our departure from India, we asked ourselves whether the intense impressions and experiences would fade once we were back home again. Perhaps we had simply succumbed to the exotic charm of the location and the fascination of this radiant, beautiful, and intelligent woman who had an extraordinary gift of expressing herself eloquently in English as well as a profound ability to understand what an individual needs at a given moment. Yet contrary to our initial skepticism, these initial experiences in the ashram had a lasting effect on both Elisabeth and me. We returned to India several times to participate in various seminars. These led us even further toward obtaining a deeper awareness of ourselves until an internal stimulus distinctly called on us to stop looking outside for that which we had already discovered within ourselves.

When I was a young man, I had a presentiment that I would do something completely different professionally when I turned fifty. After my first community-building workshop, while sitting in a New York taxi in the midst of heavy traffic, it suddenly occurred to me what this new occupation would be: I would accompany people in the development of their spiritual consciousness and in finding their true purpose relating to both their individual and community-oriented behavior.

In 1989, I was trained by Barbara Gluck as a facilitator in past-lives work, in accordance with the method she had developed in collaboration with Chris Griscom. She taught me how to accompany people in helping them to experience their inner selves, while at the same time remaining in clear contact with my own inner guidance. I learned from her that when I surrender to my inner self, I no longer have to question whether my actions are right or wrong, or good or bad, because this bond with my inner love and wisdom causes to happen precisely what should happen. The slightest attempt to do something "well" or to be "good" breaks this bond with our inner wisdom, because the desire to be something contradicts the simple truth that in our essence we already are perfect. As a result, I would be caught up in the same illusion that I was hoping to free other people from. The assumption that we are not good enough is a disease of Western civilization, and the pressure to achieve is its symptom. By yearning to be something different than what we truly are, we doom ourselves to a kind of compulsive behavior of acquiring love, status, or material belongings, which is a contradiction in itself.

This insight supported me during the therapy sessions with clients as well as in other situations, because the principle is always the same. During my professional training and within the Practice for Consciousness Development that I subsequently set up, I gained confidence in my own inner self, as well as in that of the people I was accompanying. Aided by these skills, blockages that had been acquired earlier in life could be relived, understood and released during the past life sessions. Perhaps we will never know if these previous-lifetime experiences are those of our individual soul or whether our inner self gains access to experiences stored in the collective consciousness of humanity, our culture, or our family. In any case, the distinction is insignificant since the purpose of this work is to transform patterns that restrict the individual's potential at present.

Through this process, I began to appreciate that each person recollects inner knowledge at a different pace. Everyone has a rhythm and a particular interplay between light and shadow according to his individual evolution. The resolve with which we generally judge our own limitations and those of others can give way to a more humorous perspective if we recognize these limitations as components of the individual paths toward greater consciousness. We have all picked the apple from the tree of knowledge, but how many of us have already fully digested it and landed—bang!—back home in paradise?

Within the company, I began to look at the shortcomings of my employees from this perspective. For example, it makes no sense to employ a person whose responsibilities include opening a store punctually if he has trouble getting out of bed in the morning. Instead of getting upset about such a minor offense as unpunctuality, I would try to unite the interests of the firm and the individual employee. If it were viable from an organizational point of view, such a person would be entrusted with tasks that could be performed later in the day. Otherwise, we would have to part ways. In most cases, it was not a matter of doubting the qualities of the employee but simply meant that our interests were incompatible.

Initially Peter, my cousin and business partner, was taken aback by my changed behavior. He envisioned me floating two meters off the ground and feared that it would have negative repercussions on the business. Furthermore, when I disclosed to him that I wanted to reorganize the firm with a view to gradually stepping down from my executive role and to spend more time pursuing my new professional interests, he was extremely upset. Finally, though, I was able to convince him that it was necessary to restructure the company. Until then, the firm had clearly bore the stamp of the two of us as the leading figures. If Peter and I were absent, no decisions were made. That was just the way things were. As partners, we could stand in for each other in our various tasks; we were a well-rehearsed team and knew each department and all the business procedures inside out. It was now important to make the enterprise transparent to others. Our staff, who had become accustomed to the two owners taking sole responsibility for determining the direction of the company, should take on new responsibilities. I was surprised to discover that this was by no means what everyone wanted. Apparently I had underestimated just how long such a transition takes, particularly for employees who had been part of the existing structure for many years. In the end, the reorganization took several years before it had encompassed all the departments. In hindsight, I realize that it was high time for the company to move in that direction. The antiquated management style practiced up to that point had given rise to a company that lacked the necessary flexibility to react effectively to new challenges. We needed to give the firm a new structure that would ensure its survival even after we were gone. The correlating need to find a corporate vision that could be embraced by all employees instead of simply being handed down by the management team led to the processes previously described.

The plan was that the new, commonly defined principles should gradually permeate the company and slowly but surely take hold. Information was no longer withheld or simply conveyed from top to bottom. Everyone could participate in the flow of information and communicate questions, interpretations, and analyses. In this transparent structure of interconnected circles, there were no "unimportant" positions. In a circle, each dot is connected to every other dot and contributes to the field of information. This type of awareness creates a core energy in which the whole is supported by each separate entity. In this spirit, the flow of energy reached the members of our company, our customers, and our suppliers; the new conditions influenced our overall public relations work and contributed to a healthy year-end balance sheet.

Oddly enough, Peter was not the only one who initially met my personal transformation with skepticism. During all the changes, I continually asked myself where my single-minded commitment would lead. Perhaps I was only deceiving myself and the inner guidance that I thought I was following with my entire being would turn out to be nothing more than a figment of my imagination. After all, I had spent my whole life practicing linear thinking and was unaccustomed to taking major steps. Moreover, while Peter was gradually beginning to accept the "new" corporate style and had started to think about stepping down from his management role as well, I suddenly began to have a strong sense of fear.

In 1993, Elisabeth and I purchased a stately seventeenth-century manor house in Autigny, a village in the French-speaking part of Switzerland. A year later, we were granted permission to renovate. At the company, the new structure had reached the point where Peter and I thought we could appoint a successor. We had devoted a great deal of care and thought to this matter and ultimately chose someone whom we thought incorporated musical prowess and business sense as well as an understanding for the core values of the company.

At last, everything was turning out as I had hoped. But rather than being pleased, I started to panic. As long as I had been preoccupied with implementing the changes, my fears had had no room to make themselves felt. But now everything I had set in motion had become reality all at once. It meant leaving our Zurich home of nearly thirty years to move to a new region where the language was unfamiliar to both myself and my wife and where we had hardly any friends or acquaintances. In addition, the move meant being farther away from the company, which had been put in the hands of someone whose capabilities we were not yet in the position to fully judge.

It was all a bit too much to take. What if everything turned out to be a castle in the air that would drive me and my entire family into financial ruin? At that time, my overwhelming fear about the future overrode all my faith in inner guidance. Nevertheless, if there was any meaning to everything I had experienced up to that point, I had no alternative but to continue trusting my inner guidance. I then firmly decided to have faith that nothing could happen to me that was not a part of my learning process. I would accept this process—come what may.

It was a leap into the unknown. It began with what turned out to be my final trip to Ganeshpuri. I went there with a longing to fully surrender myself to my true being, the place of absolute trust within myself, which I had lost touch with due to all the efforts of the past months, the events and the ensuing fears. Perhaps due to my inner readiness and certainly also because of the spiritual support I received in this special setting, I found this inner source, which since then I have never had cause to doubt. It is impossible for me to relate all of the experiences I had in Ganeshpuri in a way that is easy to comprehend. The following experience is just one example.

During my stay in Ganeshpuri, I worked in the temple of the deceased master Sri Baghawan Nitjananda, the teacher of the ashram's founder, Swami Muktananda. One of my tasks there included pouring a few drops of the water used the previous day to wash Nitjananda's statue into the hands of those who had made a long pilgrimage to this spiritual center of the ashram to receive Nitjananda's blessings. Sometimes people arrived by the busload and all I could see was a sea of eyes and hands—young, old, well-groomed, wrinkled, crippled leper hands and deep-set, happy, dark, questioning eyes. Dozens and dozens, one after another. Hundreds in the space of a few hours.

One day, without realizing it, I fell into a state in which I became one with all these people. Shivaratri, the annual spring festival that was held in honor of Shiva, had been celebrated all night long beyond the gates of the temple. As the people streamed into the temple after the morning chant, I became filled with an indescribable feeling of joy. The entire building was vibrating. Everything I set eyes on I perceived as being part of me; everything in the room became one. There was no before, no after, no beginning, no end, no more questions. Only joy, the present, the now.

I then understood that this experience of oneness is the ultimate aim of all our yearning. There is nothing more. Things, nature, and people we long for promise us this fulfillment. While they can provide us with temporary states of happiness, they also inevitably confront us with their impermanence. This, in the end, is their contribution toward our spiritual evolution. Eternal and unlimited happiness is to be found only in ourselves. Whenever we are fully present in the now and our thoughts are tranquil for one moment, this abundance will touch us from within. The first bite of the longed-for chocolate cake is so heavenly because it fills us with this feeling of abundance in the here and now. With the second or third bite, when our thoughts are already preoccupied with the future, we have already left happiness and abundance behind us. And we continue to strive for new things, people, or circumstances that promise us the joy of that very first bite.

A large part of the economy operates based on this misconception. The advertising industry relentlessly implies that by purchasing a new this or that, we can buy our way into paradise. Entire professions boom on the basis of recipes for success that claim they will transform us into millionaires or eternal beauties. Some teachers and gurus also present themselves as the ne plus ultra and misuse their role by producing dependence among their clientele.

Hence, a true teacher will never direct a pupil's longing toward himself, but always toward the pupil's own inner guidance. Such a teacher will encourage the pupil at all times to hold fast to the presence of his inner self.

When I decided to accept my learning processes from the heart of the now, I was thinking for the most part about dealing with external challenges. It was not yet apparent to me that my inner sanctity would confront its own shadow over and over again. However, working with our new manager soon triggered my fear of losing control. True to the parable of only seeing the splinter in the other person's eye, I recognized and challenged his shortcomings but not my own. Since he did the same, and the ensuing negative business results renewed my fear of losing my livelihood, we were at odds with each other within two years. Had I not become familiar with my consciousness, whose connectivity with everything that exists encompasses even disagreeable executives, I certainly would never have tried to pinpoint the motives of my defensive behavior.

Both the new manager and I were willing to take part in individual coaching sessions. In doing so, each of us encountered the roots of the conflict that we had triggered. Within this process, we arrived at a point where both continued collaboration and a parting of ways were potential outcomes. Independently from one another—and therefore of our own free will—we opted to end our business relationship.

During the eighteen months when our would-be successor had been running the company, I embarked on my new occupation with enthusiasm. The trip to the slum of Ibayo, which I described earlier, was one of the most important experiences and turning points for my new activities. Elisabeth and I had needed some thirty years—by way of Jungian psychology, Za-Zen, Tao yoga, spiritual experiences in India, and past-life work in the United States—to find a way to share these new facets of our personal development. We renovated our house in Autigny with the intention of it becoming a gathering place. Today, people regularly attend concerts in our music room. We have plenty of space to put up visitors who are participating in courses or who simply wish to spend a few days of quiet and reflection. And not least, the house accommodates my Practice for Consciousness Development. My desire to dedicate myself to this exchange had grown increasingly stronger.

However, after our manager resigned, I was confronted with a completely different situation. Peter divulged to me that he was no longer willing to resume his role as managing codirector of the company. Now *I* was shocked. What would become of the plans I had been trying to realize for so long? Peter, who had once so tacitly and loyally functioned alongside me, had now succeeded in distancing himself from the company—which was initially *my* idea—and was no longer ready to come when he was needed.

Here I went through another learning process, which this time, for a change, was linked with a challenge that had less to do with unresolved fears than with tangible needs. It was clear to me that if I, too, distanced myself from this situation, the company would be endangered not only idealistically but also materially. Why was my path leading me back again to managing the company? Was it because there was still something for me to discover there? Should I even be happy about this turn of events? In this context, a story from China comes to mind:

An old farmer and his son worked together cultivating their small plot of land. They had only one horse, which pulled the plough to till the fields. One day the horse ran away.

"How terrible," said the neighbors. "What bad luck."

"Who knows," answered the old farmer, "if it is good or bad luck?"

A week later, the horse returned from the hills, bringing with it five wild horses.

"How wonderful," said the neighbors. "What good luck."

"Who knows whether it is good or bad luck?" said the old man.

The next morning, the farmer's son tried to tame one of the wild horses. He fell and broke his leg.

"How awful. What bad luck," lamented the neighbors.

"Who knows whether it will bring good or bad luck?" the farmer said.

Some weeks later, soldiers marched into the village and enlisted every able-bodied youth they found there. When they saw the farmer's son with his broken leg, they let him off. He was the only one spared. Was it good luck or bad luck?

In other words, a situation that initially meets with resistance reveals its riches only if it is fully accepted. Although I needed some time to become accustomed to the idea, I realized that it would be a tremendous opportunity to manage the company on my own after having run it together with my cousin for nearly forty years. Now, finally, I would be able to give free rein to my intuition. Peter never did like to experiment. During our partnership, he was the one who always wanted to know and anticipate exactly why and how things functioned in a particular way. At first, I found his precise questions annoying and pedantic. He, in turn, pointed out how rash and imprudent I could be. Even so, in the course of our long-standing working relationship, we learned to appreciate each other's qualities and to acknowledge that they complemented our own. While he often wanted specific answers to his questions, I was able to help him see things from another, non-rational, perspective.

The music industry was undergoing radical change.

Although I finally had the opportunity to merge inner guidance and management without constraint, I still had to get by without Peter's assistance, which meant that I needed to integrate his role into my own. Many elements, such as our corporate vision, already existed and merely needed to be revitalized. Admittedly, our corporate culture and business results had to be equally convincing, particularly since Peter and I agreed that we would sell the company when the time was right. The industry of recorded music was undergoing radical change. There was no doubt in our minds that there would always be a future for music. But only younger people who were ready to devote themselves to the virtually inexhaustible possibilities offered by electronic media would be able to successfully open new opportunities in this area.

We had already started restructuring the firm before we appointed the new manager. After his departure and my reinstatement as CEO, I began to cultivate the trust and community-building process that already existed both within and between the various departments. At first, the change in management resulted in a general mood of uncertainty. I did not want to dispel these feelings by making excuses or by placing the blame on my predecessor. I saw only one way to confront this air of uncertainty and mistrust—by being authentic, by being a living example, and by using clear, open, honest communication. Furthermore, this mode of conduct should also apply to the management and to every employee vis-à-vis our customers, suppliers, and, above all, ourselves. This commitment to honesty proved to be the key to the company's new self-identity. It gave rise to the previously described forms of communication, such as the "we rounds," and injected new life into our corporate vision, which had a positive effect on the self-confidence of each individual and increased the general open-mindedness of all the employees.

This growing climate of confidence led to my handing over increasing responsibility to the divisional and departmental managers, which gradually made my presence in the firm less necessary. During the first year, I spent two to three days per week at the office. In the second year, I needed to be present only three days every fortnight. On those occasions, I spent most of my time holding talks with the management staff. Perhaps it was precisely this coming and going and the distance I gained from the various problems that enabled me to become aware of the well-worn paths and led me to develop and introduce new ideas. Sometimes my employees reacted with annoyance when I—seemingly without good reason—challenged well-established company procedures. There was already plenty to do, and naturally everyone was keen on retaining methods that had become common practice and offered them some sense of security. However, by questioning firmly rooted theories and structures, we created room for new impulses.

The entire universe revolves around the alternation between order and chaos. Modern-day physics and biology have taught us that every minute particle, in open as well as closed systems, is in constant interchange with all connected particles. Each transaction gives rise to new encounters, and nothing remains as it was before. Everything continuously "in-forms" itself over and over again.

In order not to stem the flow, there has to be confidence that even chaotic conditions within a company will reorganize themselves according to the given situation. Admittedly, this presupposes that the process is grounded in a deeper meaning—a pattern woven from shared values—that expands with each new experience while still retaining its basic form.

At this stage, I had developed enough trust in the jointly discovered meaning and purpose of our business to break away from the rules stipulating that things should be done in a certain manner simply because we had always done them that way. Even before it became clear, I could sense when such rules hindered our progress. An intuitive perception helped me to better recognize these signs and their reciprocal effect on the company organism as a whole. Consequently I was able to react before timeworn patterns became obstacles that blocked everything. As my inner sense of trust grew, I became more daring when it came to relinquishing external safeguards. I felt moved to break up structures and norms that had become a force of habit. Intuitively I felt that in doing so new, more comprehensive, and more efficient procedures would ensue. Although the employees did not always share my enthusiasm, they were ultimately the ones who ensured that the once-rigid company structure evolved into a lively organism whose individual parts were no longer mired in obsolete rules and regulations. The firm was thus able to handle new information and challenges with greater flexibility than before. After I rejoined the company, the business results once again experienced an upswing. I viewed this positive turn as a direct result of this all-encompassing process.

This success led me to the understanding that management and inner guidance are to a large extent compatible with one another. My inner guidance proved to be a substantial strength in difficult situations. By connecting to it, my perception shifted from separation and partial views to unity and integral perspectives. Thus I had discovered my inner "filling station," so to speak; while integration requires the ability to differentiate, it does not necessarily mean getting caught up in partial aspects. Taking this approach saves a tremendous amount of energy and increases efficiency. Peter, my cousin and once-skeptical business partner, also noticed my development and retracted the fears he had harbored.

I cannot and am not attempting to prove to skeptics that inner guidance exists. However, it can be experienced by opening oneself to the concept of inner listening. With awareness, we learn to discern guidance from other inner voices, and if we dare to follow their directives, we must then take a clear look at where they have led us.

In his book *The Universe Is a Green Dragon: A Cosmic Creation Story*, physicist Brian Swimme wrote: "At first there was no fireball, then it suddenly erupted. The universe erupted; all that has existence erupted out of nothing, all of being erupted into shining existence. What I would like you to understand is that this plenary emptiness permeates you. You are more fecund emptiness than you are created particles. We can see this by examining one of your atoms...Nothingness. All empty. You are more emptiness than anything else. Indeed, if all the space were taken out of you, you would be a million times smaller than the smallest grain of sand."

What if we became aware of this invisible energy, this space that, by way of its multifaceted expression, constantly recreates the diversity of being? What if we were able to perceive our true essence, at one with this all-knowingness? What if we were to immerse ourselves in this infinite abundance and become more aware of our fundamental strength? What if we were to willfully abandon ourselves to the dance of this indivisible universe?

The term "integral enterprise" would no longer sound peculiar. The economy would be shaped by people who are comfortable with integral awareness and who no longer separate subjective and objective, internal and external, consciousness and form. They would understand that each insight and development occurs within an inseparable network of relationships, in which significant and seemingly insignificant components are taken into consideration. Respect for life would be coupled with respect for oneself and one's own place in the world. Corporate ethics would not be dictated by external needs, nor would corporate behavior simply be a matter of cultivating an outer image; instead, it would be understood that sharing was a natural act necessary to bring a company's own abundance into equilibrium.

Inner guidance serves to remind us who we are, in what context we exist, and from which abundance we draw courage and hope. Our inner guidance helps us comprehend the meaning that is waiting to be discovered behind seemingly disconnected circumstances.

I, indeed, was not suffering from a lack of such circumstances. By now, Peter and I had sold the company to a firm that had approached us on its own initiative. Everything got off to a good start; the new proprietor's chain of CD retail outlets in French-speaking Switzerland complemented our network in such a way that it became the country's leading specialist in the field of CDs. We all had high hopes that the firm's young management team would place their main focus on the electronic music trade. They agreed that it made sense to continue concentrating the existing musical instrument departments in the Zurich region, sensing that the highly personal style of management and first-class craftsmanship that characterized these departments would suffer by setting up a branch network. Our corporate culture was widely accepted. I also perceived an interest on their part for me to assume an advisory role in the company's ensuing development. We finally agreed on a fair price and came to an agreement.

However, the bank issuing the loan to the new owners demanded that we make concessions regarding the payment terms of the sale. Although this annoyed us, we agreed to their demands, not wanting to jeopardize the project so close to achieving our goal. Throughout our entire business careers, we had never borrowed capital and had repaid the mortgages on all our real estate. We were now experiencing for the first time how the heavy burden of high indebtedness can weigh on the freedom of entrepreneurial decisions. The pressure to perform financially in order to be able to pay the interest rates and amortize loans created an ambience in which the uniqueness and culture of the company played second fiddle to generating short-term profits, thus jeopardizing the firm's long-term basis of existence. The staff very quickly sensed that the values that characterized their work and made the company unique were now at risk. Any advice Peter and I gave to the new management fell on deaf ears, and we were forced to acknowledge that by selling the company we had lost our influence. Consequently, we renounced our now merely cosmetic role on the board of directors, where we would have been required to make decisions we could not support.

This entire development triggered grave doubts within myself. Surely our former employees were asking themselves, "How could they both have been so blind? Why didn't they realize where this would lead? What happened to the much-touted intuition?"

Had I removed myself from the whole affair in self-interest? Had I failed? And were all the reproaches justified, including the one declaring that I had been disloyal with respect to the achievements of my ancestors? I was also concerned about my own material interests. Would I ever see the final installment of the purchase price, which was due only after full reimbursement of the bank loan? Would the company be able to continue paying the rent for the shop and office space in the buildings that still belonged to us? Then again, against the backdrop of our personal unfoldment and needs, as well as the developments in the market and in the music sector, the time of the sale was aptly chosen. We had scrutinized various potential buyers and had chosen the new owners to the best of our judgment. All internal and external factors had spoken in favor of this decision. What, however, was the meaning of this situation? Was it good luck or bad luck?

In the meantime, I was forced to question something even more fundamental. After a "routine" analysis of my blood count, I unexpectedly found myself in the waiting room of an oncologist. There I was greeted by a display of printed material offering advice for cancer patients, together with advertisements for hairpieces and headscarves. The diagnosis that I was suffering from an unusual form of leukemia struck me out of the blue. Good luck or bad luck?

I had two options: either I could despair or I could put even more faith in my inner wisdom, which in some way or another must have got me into this situation in the first place. Suddenly confronted with the fact that my life was possibly nearing its end, I was catapulted straight into what really mattered. Whatever way my path would lead, I would follow. The challenge of facing up to perhaps the most existential learning process of my life guided me toward an overall peace and serenity. The ensuing distance I gained to external problems helped me to view things from a new perspective.

It became increasingly evident that the sale of the company had encouraged the staff members to realize their own strengths. It appeared that our commonly developed corporate culture had indeed become deeply rooted among the majority of the employees, as they were able to stand up to the new management in support of these values. The employees succeeded in resisting measures that conflicted with their values and their personal integrity. They were even willing to risk their jobs for their own convictions. Some continued to discuss their feelings with me, and I was pleased to be able to support them in upholding their values.

From an outsider's point of view, however, it looked for a while as though the company would go under. Good luck or bad luck?

But what is luck? And how would evolution respond if we were to ask? Perhaps we would discover that luck lies in the plenitude of all the experiences each of us has made; that it proves itself in a constantly expanding, comprehensive consciousness that continually seeks and finds new ways in which to unfold. On doing so, it is possible that some material structures—including companies—will not survive the process, thus making room for other structures that are more viable and beneficial.

In any case, if such a development meant that I would have to face a personal material loss, I made up my mind to accept this loss as an expression of my consciousness unfoldment; just as easily as I accepted being guided to a physician who specialized in the very form of leukemia I had and who was able to cure me without my having to suffer the usual side effects of chemotherapy.

Trusting that we will always be the water of the ocean, we can ride with the waves. For years I have had a recurring dream, which I dreamed again just before we moved into our new home.

I dreamed about a junction from where it was said one could meet the One, the eternal, the all-embracing Shiva. In the dream I go to this place to meet the god Shiva, but he is not there. I stand at the junction, lonely, waiting. Nothing happens. Nothing moves. Silence. Suddenly it dawns on me: "Everything is Shiva." At that moment, in the middle of the crossing, I become part of an all-knowing, exhilarating dance.

Change of scene: I dream that I am lying in bed while raging storm winds rattle the shutters of my open window and tear my covers away. The wind lifts me up with tremendous strength. I have to hold on to the bed. I know I will be lost if I stop repeating the mantra "Om Namah Shivaya" (I surrender to the One).

I repeat the mantra over and over. The storm abates, and a tree starts to grow under my feet. It grows inside me and through me. My arms are its branches. My head is its crown. I see the tree in its entire beauty. It turns green and glows. I know I am the tree. I am Shiva.

The Integral Enterprise
or the Enterprise as a Subtle
Organism

Martina: I would like to return to the topic of evolution. We develop our-selves both collectively and individually from one stage of consciousness to the next. However, this progression is not to be understood in the sense of a ladder, where one leaves behind one step after the other while ascending. Instead, it entails integrating each stage into the next more comprehensive one. The nature of evolution is a perpetual act of transcending and embrac-ing, in which transitions and interaction flow. If I assume that we transfer the principle of our development to the systems that we design, then inevitably these consciousness levels are to be found in the structure of an enterprise.

Hans: Accordingly, there is an evolution of the organizational structures and management styles that also always reflect the life within the company. The various consciousness levels are constantly active in both the management and the open system of a company. Within a management team with inte-gral consciousness, the interaction between these levels is open and cre-ative, both internally and externally. However, if levels have been violated or if they are not sufficiently acknowledged, they are inclined to extract them-selves from the consciousness, and from the unconscious create confusion. This occurs at both an individual and a corporate level, because each com-pany is an organism in which both its various parts and its employees are individual expressions of the all-encompassing consciousness.

Perhaps our different professional experiences—that of an entrepreneur and that of an actress, author, and director—complement each other particularly well here. The nature of the integral consciousness is deeply creative. Ideally, an actor learns to differentiate the consciousness of his body from that of his feelings and to perceive the different signals without being controlled by any particular one. Bodily awareness, emotion, and thought arrive at stillness through observation. By way of this internal balance, intuition can flow freely. The actor is perhaps not always aware of this process. However, to be authentic, he must have access to intuition.

Hamlet's speech to the Players expresses this in a different manner: "Use all gently; for in the very torrent, tempest, and, as I may say, the whirlwind of passion, you must acquire and beget a temperance that may give it smoothness...For anything so overdone is from the purpose of playing, whose end, both at the first and now, was and is to hold, as 'twere, the mirror up to nature, to show virtue her own feature, scorn her own image, and the very age and body of the time his form and pressure" (Shakespeare's *Hamlet*, act 3, scene 2).

The attentiveness Hamlet seeks here results from the ability to observe. In order to observe nature in the reflection of the water, the water must be still. Pure observation is able to calm thoughts, feelings, and physical sensations. In this conscious state of being, there is neither past nor future—only the present.

In his book *The Open Door*, director Peter Brook refers to this as entering a still relationship with one's deepest self, in the place where meaning arises. Sometimes we speak of an actor giving a soul to his role. Opening oneself up to the intuitive, spiritual dimension gives a soul and a meaning not only to theater productions. In the end, we are all players acting out our beliefs and convictions, our values and qualities. But does this mean that our portrayal is thus also endowed with a soul?

It is not our intention here to give our readers a lesson in acting. Rather, on the following pages we will deal with a holistic understanding of our strengths of consciousness and how they are reflected in the management style of a company.

Executives of integral enterprises are aware of the interdependence of their feelings, thoughts, words, and actions with the state of society and the planet. In other words, they understand the earth as a superordinate enterprise, a collective organism, of which they are a part. They recognize themselves as a piece of the whole, which in turn is a piece of an even larger whole, and so on ad infinitum. The secret of their strength lies precisely in this conscious cooperation. They are neither separated from the rest of the world nor do they perceive themselves as such.

They are guided by a vision that is based on the role of their company within a life-enhancing economy. A company's vision is a message supported by all the "players" involved. It creates a fundamental vibration that takes hold of and shapes the whole. In other words, it gives a soul to the company and frees its managers from the hubris of thinking that they have to do everything on their own. The inspired vision allows them to be part of a dynamic cooperation, where their task is to continually perceive and integrate. If they aim to enforce corporate goals, they will destroy this subtle web of creative cooperation. The trend of awarding executives the title of Manager of the Year arises from the notion of one "strong man" who can single-handedly steer a company toward success. But where do managers get the inspiration for their thoughts and actions? In other words, could a director put on a play without any actors?

He could not. Collectively discovering and creating, rejecting, releasing, reinventing, opening up, getting involved, abandoning, and becoming conscious of both oneself and one's role—all this belongs to the artistic landscape on the stage, and similarly it applies to the creative process of integral leadership. After all, in companies, too, new plays are constantly being produced and new roles are being assigned all the time. To this end, first of all an empty space— an empty "stage"—is needed within the manager, free of old concepts, old sets, and old props.

It is only in the reflection of still water or in the empty space of the self that we are able to perceive the presence of all our internal facets and strengths, the shadow and the light, our existence as human beings.

In this sense, everyone is his own stage director. The question is, though, whether we are aware of the inner strengths of our consciousness and whether we are able to lead the way. Let us assume that the "play" is called consciousness realization; our work as director subsequently consists of discovering the forms and roles of these physical, emotional, rational, and intuitive strengths, becoming acquainted with and vitalizing them, and harmonizing their various potentials, mentalities, and roles. In other words, the director acts as a keen observer and intermediary of the entire spectrum with which he is presented.

Once we assume the direction, that is, the responsibility, for our own internal life, we generally manage to accept responsibility in our external realm of activities as well.

However, applying this idea to a company, we are much less accustomed to regarding it as a delicate structure that reacts to subtle influences. No one can read another person's thoughts and feelings. Yet we know that thoughts and feelings are real, as real as the table we sit at or the food we eat.

During my final years working as an entrepreneur, I sought intensively for ways to unite my deep inner experiences with a vital, external form of the company. At the same time, I came across a book written by the management consultant Rudolf Mann entitled *Das ganzheitliche Unternehmen* (The Holistic Enterprise), and I subsequently attended one of the author's workshops of the same name. Straightaway, Mann was able to provide me with a genuine understanding of holistic management nurtured by a spiritual perspective. When he talked about a company also having a "subtle" body, everything became clear to me. I had waited for just this image—a living corporate organism endowed with different characteristics of consciousness. Its earthing, the material foundation of the company consists of assets and liabilities, property and debt. A solid company capital is the core of its subsistence; overindebtedness signals the end.

The next layer, still physical but considerably more versatile, is formed by operational activities: customer flow, orders, production, services, and income and expenditure. Their relationships to each other lead to either profit or loss. Correspondingly, in the human body this layer is to be found in the vegetative nervous system, which controls all vital bodily functions, such as food metabolism.

Emotions and thoughts are part of the subtle fabric of being human. We can also find these subtle manifestations in certain spheres of a company. The emotions of a company convey themselves through its charisma: enthusiasm, joy, passion for one's work, and an affinity for other people all attract customers and employees. Effective public relations and advertising are expressions of this. The rational potential enables us to focus our strengths on values and objectives in our structuring and planning activities. And what I felt was missing in Mann's concept of a corporate organism, I found in philosopher Jean Gebser's understanding of evolution—an awareness of all physical, emotional, and rational potential and its integration into a more comprehensive consciousness.

In this integral consciousness, I experience myself as the observer of my material and subtle expression. I observe my body, my feelings, and my thoughts without becoming entrapped in their respective expressions. It is an awareness that leads me to the realization of being part of a larger whole.

Everyone can recreate this experience in a simple stillness exercise. If I were only my body, how would I be able to perceive it? If I were no more than my feelings and thoughts, how could I witness them? From the integral perspective, I am aware of my different levels of consciousness with their individual needs, and I am able to respond to them from a more comprehensive context.

In practice, I learned from Mann, above all, how much more sensible it is to change a company from an immaterial perspective of visions and ideas rather than merely at the material level. The latter requires the efforts of Hercules, toiling where only a part of the whole is visible in its most dense materialization. The level at which shortcomings become evident is not necessarily that at which they originally developed. Although this may seem quite obvious, during a crisis it is common practice to potter around at one level, namely the material one.

Here too the human body provides a fitting analogy. Thanks to my therapeutic training and increasing practical experience, I know that repressed emotions and rigid thoughts manifest themselves in the body and inhibit the flow of energy. Subsequently, such blockages can lead to all types of diseases. A treatment that deals only with the body does not always yield the desired lasting result. Often, these clogging energy structures can only be located and vitalized with the help of the inner guidance of the client, because they are hidden from the direct reach of the rational mind. If, however, the repressed "spirits" are encouraged by the inner self to express themselves, they can also be understood and—if the time is right—transformed. Once connected to his inner self, the client reassumes the direction on the internal "stage."

With time, I learned how to use life-energy healing methods to balance my clients' minor health problems. I noticed the effectiveness of a treatment regardless of my spatial distance to the recipient. These experiences aroused the researcher in me. I asked myself whether the different consciousness fields that operate within a company or any other institution could be nourished and balanced from a distance.

> *As if I were holding the company in my hands,*
> *I opened myself and attempted*
> *to perceive and balance its subtle body.*

Thus I began to experiment with my company as I had learned to do with human beings. As if I were holding the company in my hands, I opened myself and attempted to perceive and balance its subtle body.

First I attended to the physical realms; I visualized the financial health of the company, our well-maintained business premises with a lively flow of customers, and its smoothly running operational procedures. Then I imagined the aspects that embodied the emotional consciousness of the enterprise—the radiation of joy and readiness to serve that emanated from the staff and from everything else that represented us to the outside world.

Next, I devoted myself to the "brain" of the enterprise, the rational structures through which our various lines of business and departments oriented their tasks and their internal interplay. Finally, I focused on the company potential and saw it in the light of a more comprehensive, all-pervading consciousness field. This is where meaning and purpose, the reason for the company to exist, are contained.

During this subtle examination, to my surprise the managers in charge of the areas of the company that I had conjured up immediately appeared in my inner vision. It was not my intention to request anything specific from these employees. Instead, I yielded to my inner wisdom and trusted that its energy would flow exactly where it was needed. This conscious interaction with my inner guidance meant that I had to bow again and again to the principle of "Thy will be done." Through this "live and let live" attitude, I experienced how much faster and more accurately the triggering point for changing a given situation within the enterprise could be found. As a result, we saved both time and energy, which had previously been wasted on overcoming resistance, mostly self-induced.

I discovered that decisions made along these lines showed greater compassion and increasingly became more persuasive and effective. A new understanding of relevancy—indeed, life enhancement—ensued. By using this approach, I sensitized my perception to the different needs within the company in a completely new way. And perhaps it was even thanks to this method that the company required less of my presence than ever before. It is hard to say whether this procedure was directly responsible for the positive development within the firm, or whether the clarity and balance that it brought about in my own behavior then carried over to the company. Or maybe it was a combination of both these factors.

The film director Helmut Käutner once said that he sees his relationship with his actors as that of a gardener. The image of a gardener also sprung to mind when, in the course of the vision process at the firm, I examined my own role within the company. In my mind's eye, I saw a flower garden and realized that it was my task to sense what was needed for the plants to thrive, to perceive their blossoms, and to take pleasure in them. Although it was a rather unspectacular image, it helped me to understand that it was important, in an integral sense, to perceive how the vision or the purpose vitalizes each and every cell of the company and therefore the firm as a whole.

Perceiving the company as a garden, an organism, and preserving it as a blossoming image in my mind helped me to align myself with its qualities and possibilities instead of attaching too much importance to mistakes and shortcomings. I practiced recognizing and "treating" obstructions in the energy flow of the company just as I would in myself, namely, with acceptance and compassion.

The global economy as a whole, however, still seems to be a long way off from perceiving the world, let alone a company, in the way a thoughtful gardener does his own garden. And yet the evolution of consciousness already places a privileged part of mankind in a position to do so.

At the beginning of this book, we mentioned that we hold the entire chain of information that led to the creation and expansion of the universe within ourselves. Stardust, as it were, has been clinging to us since time immemorial. Compared with this long chain of being, our emergence into existence and the comprehensible development of consciousness up to the present time constitute only a tiny fraction of the whole. However, humans, as an expression of this evolutionary development, have the ability to contemplate and be aware of it. We are the universe, or rather the entire evolution, both in its material and biological form and in its consciousness. A person can look at his development in the same way a gardener views his garden from the window of his house.

Using Christian mythology as an analogy, the consciousness evolution of humans began in paradise, in the Garden of Eden, in the primordial, but still unconscious, oneness of being. When God gave man a companion and both Adam and Eve ate from the tree of the knowledge, they were driven out of this unconscious oneness (unconscious because they knew nothing else). This expulsion from paradise marks the beginning of the path of the worldly experience of mankind, as well as of each and every human life. The pain of separation from oneness is the root of primordial fear, rage, and unworthiness. It results in the world being divided up into good and evil, angels and devils. The unconscious longing for unity drives humans into an ever-deeper enmeshment with the illusionary permanence of property, security, and relations. Only on reaching a dead end in delusion does the encapsulated "I" give in and ask itself about the meaning of life. By posing this question, we may arrive at a new understanding of our personal circumstances. By understanding the nature of the forces that got us into this entanglement, and through the possibility of integrating these forces, we become increasingly aware of our true nature. Compassion for oneself and all others grows from the ultimately enlightening experience of losing oneself in the illusion of outer manifestation. Thus the circle closes; the mythological representation of paradisiacal oneness gives rise to the notion that the "tree of life" is still waiting to be discovered.

In order to better understand ourselves, it makes sense to take a closer look at the different stages of the evolution of our collective consciousness. Sometimes our language seems limited when it comes to describing the unfoldment of the entire consciousness spectrum that is at our disposal. If we see it as a spiral lying in front of us, it uniformly widens out into a continuously expanding circle, both horizontally and vertically. However, the term "consciousness level" suggests a ladder, which draws a parallel to the old, linear way of thinking. If we nevertheless use it, it serves merely as an aid to differentiate between the respective consciousness levels and their inherent potentials. To be more precise, what is meant here are currents that mutually determine and permeate each other. Every individual, every company, and every society is moved by different currents or conditions; cognition, identity, morality, social relations, spirituality, creativity, and so on can be developed to completely different degrees. Hence consciousness levels should not be understood as closed vessels, but rather as gravitational centers in a flowing organism. If we regard life as a spiral-shaped, continuous development, then the larger loops of the spiral indicate a more comprehensive perception in relation to the narrower ones.

Pierre Teilhard de Chardin, among others, and in particular Jean Gebser in his work *The Ever-Present Origin* and Ken Wilber have helped us to gain a better understanding of this. Wilber has, to our way of understanding, comprehensively deciphered the sphere of consciousness evolution, including cultural and spiritual traditions, like no other philosopher before him. Following Wilber's example, we have also adopted the image of the spiral and its development levels from the consciousness researchers Don Beck and Christopher Cowan (*Spiral Dynamics: Mastering Values, Leadership and Change*). Because we are concerned here with integral business, we can apply these views in the form of an analogy to the various aspects of a company. In doing so, it is important to point out the connection between collective and individual consciousness evolution and the development of behavioral patterns and leadership styles in the business world. In this connection, you will find a comparative excursus in the appendix of this book.

Assessing a company based merely on its visible, material appearance would be like judging the character of a person by his clothes. Each enterprise is a sensitive, subtle organism, the nature of which constitutes the firm's individuality and its appeal to employees, customers, partners, and the public alike. As with every organism, its health, vitality, and ability to regenerate is derived from dynamic interaction with its environment. Trying to hinder this interaction out of fear of encountering uncontrollable situations would mean severing this organism from impulses that are essential for its survival in a changing world.

A corporate vision that is not aimed at short-term gains, but instead is part of a comprehensive, socially beneficial purpose, provides the stabilizing effect of an underlying current even in times of acute economic crisis. It is precisely in times of chaos that the vision serves as an attractor around which a new and more credible structure can form. Challenges need to be embraced rather than rejected if the familiar adage "crisis as chance" is to be more than just empty words.

Taking on challenges requires having the courage to attend to every reaction of the consciousness structure, first those within one's own inner self and subsequently those within the corporate community (see the excursus in the appendix). If the personal and institutional inner life are understood and thereby come to peace, the nature of the crisis and the coinciding forces will disclose themselves. In most cases, the composition of the knot reveals the way to untie it.

At this stage, we are in the position to perceive and understand our conflict partners and what motivates them in an integral way. If we can accept them at the point where they are most agitated by acknowledging our own inclination to react emotionally, we can contribute to examining the knot together, which enables us to find a solution instead of simply cutting through it with an ax.

A company has as many unconscious parts as we do. Perhaps within the company's history there are also traumatic aspects, taboo subjects, and their resulting painful experiences, which are avoided, neglected, or not discussed. Issues that have not been addressed vanish into the shadows and develop a momentum of their own, which in turn affects the stability and charisma of the entire company. Just as external circumstances can stir up our wounds lurking in the shadows, repressed issues in a company can become painfully noticeable if provoked by the outside world. And just as an individual resists accepting the outside world as feedback of his internal world, the company runs the risk of projecting such internal blockages outwardly. As a result, critical media, dissatisfied customers, the government, and competition are seen as the enemy, and they are cursed and combated.

Then again, all human dramas take place within ourselves. Logically we should really ask ourselves: Which of our internal dormant fears are pointed out to us by external "enemies"? Do they have a shape? What do they emanate? What do they look like? How do they behave? How do we deal with them? Can we accept them? What are their needs? Giving shape to these internal forces of consciousness makes it possible to respect and release them from their existence in the shadows. By being respectfully aware of our fears, we deprive them of their power over us. Once they are acknowledged, they can be accepted and integrated, for that which no longer frightens us within ourselves can no longer frighten us in the outside world.

Leaders who are ready to accept themselves entirely, with all their loved and unloved traits, instead of excluding certain areas of their personality out of fear, will have an integrating effect on their outside realm in a similar way.

They know that fleeing from their own emotions leads to a purely rational, mechanical manner of thinking, to cold and unrelated decisions, to aggressive or defensive behavior, and—in the long run—to failure.

Each company is a sensitive, subtle organism. The perception of an integral team of leaders embraces the whole spectrum—the entire depth and width—of the consciousness spiral of the company: internally and externally, individually and collectively. Integral leadership works toward achieving an integral company, a company that assumes its individual and meaningful role in the context of a global economy, an economy that is beneficial to life.

Then the manager no longer strives primarily toward fulfilling the parameters that promise the highest possible personal income. Instead, the manager is conscious of performing a service, which is about sharing abilities, knowledge, and resources—in other words, about sharing abundance. Understood in this way, sharing creates a balance and an exchange, which encourages whatever is needed to maintain a healthy company to flow back into it.

In the same way that an integral leader will regularly retreat from day-to-day business activities in order to attend to his own balance of consciousness, including its physical, emotional, and rational elements, the material and subtle aspects of the company also long for awareness and affection. By this way of perception, the company reveals itself as a dynamic and sensitive organism. Its uniqueness is due to the many facets of the consciousness potential pulsating within it. These facets are reflected in the individual gifts and talents of the employees, who are attracted and motivated by the firm's purpose. When, at all levels, people whose focal area of consciousness is in resonance with their tasks are at work, the ideal conditions for internal and external communication arise.

Whenever We Talk about the World, We Are Talking about Ourselves

Hans: Painful conflicts are cropping up everywhere in the world, heralding radical changes. No one will be able to escape them. The more tightly we hold on to outdated patterns and structures, the more painful it will be when they fall apart.

Martina: That reminds me of a slogan I read on a highway billboard: "Don't swear about the traffic jam. You are the traffic jam."

Hans: The evolution of the collective consciousness is reflected in the development of each individual. Each one of us is important, because we are both a whole in its own right and a part of the embracing organism known as mankind at the same time.

Martina: Do you still remember your original question: What purpose does one's own transformation have within the process of Creation?

Isn't this more a question about our own significance? What do we really know about the dimension of the process of Creation? Where do we come from and where are we going? Each answer gives rise to new questions. And with each ending comes a new beginning. The air that we have just inhaled leaves our body the very next moment and is perhaps breathed in by someone else. From time to time, we are only too aware of this, for example, when we are in a restaurant and our nostrils are filled with the pungent smell of cigar smoke. Do we, every time we exhale, also send our mental state out into the world? In any case, we do not know which direction the air we have exhaled will go, what encounters it will make, and what it will trigger during these encounters.

Why does it seem so much easier for us to understand that we cannot control our breathing, while we believe the opposite about our lives? Does our life not behave like a living organism, in which small impulses can generate far-reaching, unexpected consequences? In the same way, while we accept the fact that mankind is interconnected worldwide via technology and telecommunications, we still find it unsettling that in this global organism, unforeseen consequences have a much more rapid and drastic effect on us all. We never know what is going to happen next. In the past, we did not know either, but it was easier to harbor the illusion that we did.

In face of the rapid changes in our living conditions, how do we succeed in abandoning our old control and reaction mechanisms that can no longer cope with the external diversity?

We do not expect the engine of a car to accelerate to one hundred kilometers per hour while we are still driving in first gear; instead, we shift into a higher gear. Indeed, what would be the effect on the world if an increasing number of people "shifted into a higher gear," in which their potential could be more comprehensively expressed despite the rapid changes in living conditions? What if we were to mature in our consciousness to create greater integration, compassion, and simplicity to the same degree that material evolution is becoming increasingly complex?

We constantly concern ourselves with things that are not part of the now. If we succeed in letting go of the pains of the past, and with them our worries about the future, only the present remains. In the present, the past, with its painful experiences, loses its power over our lives and can be transformed. Only in the now can we imagine and shape the potential of the future.

Long before our time, there were people who made systematic use of this wisdom. In the second month of each year, Shun, the legendary Chinese emperor, traveled to the eastern provinces to gain his own impressions of the conditions in his enormous empire. He did not do this by examining books, listening to personal accounts and matters of concern, or asking the opinion of the people. Instead, he had the local musicians play for him and paid particular attention to the fine-tuning of the various instruments. Even much earlier the legendary emperor Fu Hsi (ca. 2850 BC), to whom the book *I-Ging* is attributed, is said to have referred to music as "fu-lài," meaning "to make things possible," and "li-pen," that is, "to prepare the ground." It can therefore be assumed that music in ancient China was perceived as an invisible matrix heralding impending events.

The five tones of traditional Chinese music stand for the five elements, earth, metal, water, fire, and air; for the four points of a compass and their central point; for the four seasons and the time of year as the background; and for a political structure comprising material goods, state affairs, the people, the ministers, and the emperor as the focal point.

A Chinese legend tells of the music master Wen, who ran his fingers over the four outer strings of his zither without making a sound. He did not dare to pluck these strings until after years of practicing when he discovered—from the depth of his very being—their relationship with the fifth string and its fundamental tone, Kung. It was only from this deep-rootedness that he ventured to sound out the tones representing the four aspects of man—his physical body, his emotions, his practical mind, and his abstract mind.

This legend is an excellent analogy for orienting our manner of thinking, feeling, and acting toward our inner wisdom, because the story implies that inner wisdom only fully reveals itself if all our strengths of consciousness are perceived and integrated. According to Chinese tradition, harmony in society was also based on compliance with the absolute order. The musical tone was the intermediary between the absolute and manifest world. While a discord of the overall tone indicated forthcoming chaos and decline, the accord of the tone structure with the universal order constituted the indispensable prerequisite for harmony and stability.

The fundamental Kung tone served as the key to this harmonization. Instruments were tuned to this note. Its pitch could not be rigidly fixed; it—

and consequently the overall sound of the five-tone series—altered according to the changing times. Those listening to it were swiftly alerted to imminent external changes. However, all attempts to give circumstances any degree of permanence by codifying the tones were doomed to failure from the start.

This does not apply just to bygone days in China. The impossibility of cementing things that were once proven also applies today and in our part of the world. And it applies to companies too. Everything that we want to set in stone, be it organizational structures or plans, will fall apart sooner or later (and in today's rapidly changing world, it is more likely to be sooner than later), and the tighter we hold on to them, the more painful the change will be for us. In contrast, going with the flow involves listening to the fundamental tone of the instrument—that is, the company—and its circumstances. The corporate vision serves as the basic fifth string on which the fundamental tone becomes audible. The only reliable way to orient oneself in chaotic conditions is by aligning oneself with the corporate vision. Embodied in all the employees, it acts as a fundamental vibration that cushions external blows and enables the company to tune into new situations in a flexible manner.

I experienced the gift of hearing the quality or the nature of the moment and how it expresses itself in the fine-tuning of the instrument while working with two leading artists of Indian music—Ustad Nasir Zahiruddin Dagar and his brother, Ustad Nasir Faiyazuddin Dagar. After meeting the Dagar brothers together with some of my friends in Delhi, I invited them to Switzerland to play in concerts and to make some recordings. They upheld a family tradition in which the most ancient style of classical Indian music, Dhrupad, has been passed on and preserved by their ancestors for over twenty generations. Barely familiar with their music, I wanted to know, as soon as they had arrived in Zurich, which raga—a melodic form in Indian classical music—they had in mind for the recordings. They shook their heads in astonishment. It was not the appropriate time to think about this. I also received no response to my question when I picked them up at the hotel on the day of the recording. The same thing happened when our recording engineer descended on them with the same question upon their arrival at the studio. When would they know? "When we are tuning the tanpuras," they replied. Only from the sound of the strings would they be able to detect which raga related to the moment and wanted to be heard. They spent a considerable amount of time tuning their instruments and then, without any further deliberation, announced which raga they would play for us.

Perhaps you know the feeling: you are just about to deliver a lecture and know exactly what you want to say, but the moment you start talking, you feel that the words are running into a void. What should you do? Just keep going and read from your notes? Or do you pause to reflect for a moment? Perhaps you also communicate your feelings openly and thereby give them space just to be. Maybe then a question arises within you or one is asked by someone in the audience, which might even draw a line back to where you started. Whatever happens, it takes courage to accept the moment as it is, particularly if it is initially not what you had anticipated.

The state of not knowing prepares the ground
on which something new can grow.

It is precisely the state of not knowing that prepares the ground on which something new can grow. Sidestepping it and grasping for quick solutions and recipes for success is simply a repetition of the repetition. Fear of loss and failure causes us to make decisions, which against this backdrop only trigger new fears. The courage to embrace the now leads us toward abundance, even if we initially experience emptiness, confusion, and not knowing.

Anyone who contends that economic success and inner abundance cannot go hand in hand is mistaken. Only when I look back do I realize how much the success of the Jecklin music business was based on sharing abundance with the music world. This was due not only to the richness of our assortment—whether of instruments, CDs, scores, or musical accessories—but first and foremost to our competent employees, who created their range with great care and attention and, out of their inner motivation, provided their customers with expert advice. The core of these characteristics, which is something one might anyway expect from a specialty store, stemmed from two aspects of purpose anchored in the employees' consciousness: their understanding of the social value of music and their consequent self-respect for their role in serving this value. Against this backdrop, numerous services thrived that were not directly geared toward making a profit. Precisely because of their unintentional purpose, these services had paved the way to the company's unique touch: annual nationwide meetings for youth orchestras, ensembles, and soloists, a project that had been initiated by our fathers; a CD edition that helped Swiss musicians and composers to become recognized internationally by its presence in CD stores and in the press as far away as Tokyo and Los Angeles; a forum with one hundred seats offering Zurich's music scene an intimate setting for concerts, lectures, and courses; and countless little things, all of which gave great pleasure to everyone concerned.

Needless to say, all these activities cost money, and ultimately this was reflected in our prices. As a result, in our CD stores we were often confronted with customers who had compared our prices with those of our rivals and criticized ours for being much higher. This did not fail to irritate our employees and, for a short while, we even felt wronged by the cut-price stores. Yet we continued to focus on our strengths and the uniqueness of our company and decided to take responsibility for our prices, as well as for our services and their costs. As a result, by the end of the 1990s, Jecklin had the highest CD prices in the country. Nonetheless, we were not only the number one address for music lovers in all the locations where we had an outlet, but we were also the market leader in CD sales in terms of volume.

Outer abundance can only arise from inner abundance. Our activities emerged from the employees' enthusiasm for music, from their and our joy in being involved in something meaningful that was in tune with the needs of society. We had found our fundamental tone. The magnetism of the company resulted from its essence and from its lived vision. It was sufficient to share this abundance. This met with a positive response, and thus the material circle, without which no company can exist, closed.

If economic success and corporate community are synchronous with the inner abundance on the part of the individual employees, it is then also not too hard to imagine the possibility of a world community whose united potential works toward the common good.

It is not our intention in this book to state endless facts or make proposals relating to global change in order to underscore our view of the world. Those who do not share our experiences can probably provide just as many examples to "prove" their own worldview. We are all losers in the battle for the unambiguity of external truths, because we lose ourselves in this battle. Therefore, whenever we talk about the world, we might just as well be talking about ourselves. "What is the purpose of economy?" implies the question "What is the purpose of life?" Once this question has been posed, it can have the same effect as the prince's kiss in *Sleeping Beauty*. The potential to wake up and recognize the world as a place for enhancement despite, and precisely because of, its restrictions lies in the pursuit of the vision.

We look upon the world with the vision that we have adopted for our own lives, and are apparently only able to benefit from the potential offered by the possible developments that we perceive within ourselves. If we have the vision of a global community, we also experience it in relationship to ourselves. A peaceful interaction of the physical, emotional, and rational powers of consciousness within ourselves shapes the values, perceptions, and notions relating to everything around us.

Moreover, our ability to enter into global life-enhancing relationships develops from the life-enhancing relationship we have with ourselves. The more intimate this relationship is, the more meaningfully we interrelate and the better we will be able to integrate differences, thereby supporting each other and encouraging one another to share our special talents, visions, and material values with the world. Whether it concerns nations, cultures, or interest groups, sharing means partnership and growth for all involved, including the global economy.

It takes courage to recognize the freedom that is inherent in the restrictions that are part of everyday life. It takes courage to live according to one's own vision without setting conditions that postpone realizing the vision to a "more appropriate" time. But it is possible—both for us as individuals and together, for ourselves and for the world.

We dare to say this because courage abandons us just as often as we find it again, because Hans knows just as much about need in financial affluence as Martina understands about abundance in material limitations.

Appendix

CONSCIOUSNESS LEVELS WITHIN A COMPANY

Employee orientation   Characteristics

I as an expression of the ONE   Conscious universal order

Responsibility for oneself   Integrative and open
and the community   systems

Performance orientation   Goals and structures

Emotional creativity   Hero myths

Self-preservation   Survival instinct

Pathfinder   Healthy finances

Protection-providing patron   Tradition-consciousness

Result-oriented manager   Performance

Shaper   Service to the community

Visionary   Sharing life on the planet

Leader orientation   Company orientation

Consciousness levels   **Consciousness of
                                               oneself and the world**

Archaic   Vegetative

Material   Survival

Mythical   Group affiliation

Rational   Power of reasoning

Integral   Compassion for oneself
                                               and for others

Spiritual   Unconditional love

Appendix A
Excursus: The Dynamics of the Consciousness Spiral in Business

Preliminary remark: We have chosen the names of the stages, or "waves," of consciousness in order to unite various models (in particular those of Mann, Teilhard de Chardin, Gebser, Wilber, Beck, and Gowan), as well as to express our understanding of the effect they have within a company.

In the *material-archaic consciousness* of early humans, who over the course of millions of years have become differentiated from apes, the lives of the early hunters and gatherers were instinctively interwoven with the environment and primarily characterized by impulses for survival (eating, drinking, seeking protection from the elements and wild animals, reproducing). This consciousness is comparable to the individual development of the fetus in the womb or of the newborn child.

Here we also find the archetypical link with protozoan and earlier forms of existence—a source of elementary vitality and strength, whose injuries from the conflicts with the norms of today's society are responsible for numerous neurotic phenomena in the individual. In a company, the dominance of this consciousness leads to exclusive focusing on material property. If this is directly threatened, it triggers impulsive and shortsighted actions.

On the other hand, in the integrated material-archaic consciousness, the sensitive "gathering" nose of management that "knows where the money comes from" and perceives material opportunities or risks early on can have a helpful and complementary effect. If, however, these instinct-steered "follow me, quick march" orders lack a broader perspective, the management will quickly fail in this rapidly changing world. Managers' impulses become completely unpredictable if they are shaped by fear for survival; their style of leadership becomes even more defensive and more dictatorial. And that which leaders cannot give to themselves is missed even more by those being led: nurturing, loving affection.

Teilhard de Chardin postulated an evolutionary pull toward an increased complexity of human socialization as a continuation of the physical and biological evolution of holons into ever more comprehensive holons (from particles to atoms to molecules to organisms, and so on). The word *holon* is used to describe a basic unit of organization in biological and social systems. The development of incoherent survival hordes into tribal communities is, in this sense, one of the substantial achievements of the *material-magic consciousness*: based on blood relationships and family ties, which grant protection and security in an unfamiliar outside world, nomadic hunters and gatherers settled and became herdsmen and gardeners.

Material survival remained a key element. But it had now become dependent on the influence of higher powers, which needed to be appeased by means of worship and rituals, including human sacrifice. A magical world with matriarchal features, determined by the faith in ancestral and natural spirits, and in good and evil omens, determined the fate of both the individual and the community.

In terms of individual unfoldment, this consciousness corresponds to the stage of the infant when it discovers its own physicalness while still being strongly intertwined with the emotional states of the mother.

The corresponding aspect in the corporate consciousness is connected with the vegetative life. In view of the unpredictability of constant external change, the close bonds within a group, which form due to sharing a common destiny, promise protection and harmony.

The unfamiliar outside world does not just consist of competitors, government, or media; ultimately, every company depends on the favor of its customers. How quickly does this dependency lead to defense mechanisms, such as when being confronted with complaints, that drive the customer away forever? (Such was the case with the employee participating in the workshop titled "Joy in Serving"; when asked what gave him the greatest satisfaction, he answered, "When I can prove to the customer that he is wrong." See chapter 5, "The Vision as a Fundamental Wave within the Enterprise.") A management that identifies with the magical consciousness is inclined to secure its power by

means of favoritism. Similar to the way in which, in the collective development, tribes were formed, cliques or clans can develop within companies. The
development of the concept of enemies is characteristic of the consciousness
of cliques or clans, because internal coherence is strengthened by creating an
external opponent.

Unwritten behavioral codes and ritualized symbols of affiliation, such as com-
pany-specific attire, are used as a means of holding the clan together and dis-
tinguishing it outwardly from its rivals. The fetish of brand names on clothing
also has its origin here. Companies profit from the fact that young people, in
particular, use brand names to identify themselves. The emergence of cult
brands with high "emotional value" and correspondingly high turnover can
often be attributed to a skillful use of Levy-Bruhl's "participation mystique"
phenomenon, the objective of which is to produce a dependence on the sense
of belonging (e.g., the Marlboro feeling, emotions associated with cars and
their brands, and so on).

In management, rewards with positions of power and material prosperity, or
the threat of their revocation, lead to favoritism. Cliques within the company
make important decisions among themselves, thus destroying the motivation
of the other employees. Are not exorbitant executive salaries based on the clan
mentality, which extends beyond the boundary between the board of directors
and the management?

If material-magic consciousness is integrated, groups form based on natural
attraction and similar interests and tasks. Instead of excluding, groups have a
stabilizing and vitalizing effect on the corporate culture. It is helpful to have
the talent to recognize emotionally charged situations with a sensitive awareness and to deal with them spontaneously and empathetically.

Looking back at the two materially characterized waves of evolution, I recall
the owner of a well-known retail company who, on the busiest days before
Christmas, could not resist personally standing behind the cash register. His
apparent sensual relationship with receiving the paper money and coins
seemed to give him a feeling of security, and his employees and business colleagues called him "the numismatist." Not all manifestations of the unconscious interwoven with the early waves of our consciousness are as endearing
as those of this eccentric coin collector. Within each of us, as well as within

companies, all the levels we have experienced are active at all times in a more or less conscious way, and are helpful as well as inhibiting.

The transition to *mythical-emotional consciousness* represents an increase in the individual's ability to create boundaries between himself and the group and the environment. The development of the plough in the shift from gardening to agriculture constituted a turning point that brought with it far-reaching social consequences. According to Erich Neumann in his work *The Great Mother*, this tool, which requires two strong hands, symbolizes the separation from the psychological-matriarchal evolutionary phase and the start of the development of a patriarchal world, the beginning of history as we know it. Joseph Campbell, the leading American myth researcher, also aptly noted that the simulation of coitus with the plough, which breaks open the earth, became a dominating mythical figure (*The Power of Myth*).

Cultivation of the soil resulted in surplus, which expanded the spatial area of activity of the group and took people away from their home environment to engage in nationwide commercial activity. Tribal leaders extended their power and laid the foundations for powerful realms, such as those of the Sumerians, Egyptians, Mayans, Aztecs, and Mongols.

In a world characterized by myths about monsters, heroes, robbers, knights, and fearless conquerors, powerful feudal lords provided protection in return for subjugation and work.

In the sphere of individual personality development, this level of consciousness reflects the powerful and uncontrolled outburst of emotional self-expression, which can be observed in children at first when they reach the defiant age and later in the rebellious youth. The "I" discovers its power and wants to sound it out by having confrontations with its environment.

From this stage, the adult develops the courage to take risks, the power of resistance, and a vital and liberating creativity, provided that these strengths have not been suppressed and substituted with irreconcilability and destructive behavior.

The mythical hero who conquers all monstrous creatures is reflected in the image of the "strong man" who will lead a company out of crisis entirely on his own, as well as in the creative genius, who never fails to surprise his own environment and the competition with his continual stream of new creations. If such a genius, in all his grandiosity, underestimates the complexity of present day circumstances, he will fail pitifully as a "lone warrior." However, as a creative leader of a team he can be of inestimable value.

Under the guidance of the creative genius, the enterprise then unfolds its charisma, both externally and internally, in the form of credible advertising, public relations activities, and corporate culture.

The impetuous, emotional, and egoistical forces provoked the need for order and justice. At the *mythical-conformist stage*, limits were set on unruly and inconsiderate emotionality. Rules, behavioral standards, and laws were established. Secular and religious hierarchies determined the social coherence in the name of a higher, mythologically established order. People who shared a faith, ethos, or legal system became citizens of one nation. In the Western world, the height of this epoch extended from about 1000 BC until the Enlightenment.

In regard to human development, the child at this point experiences the transition from being an impulsive egocentric to integrating into society, with all its rules and norms. Here, in the best case, the child acquires a sense of purpose, meaning, and orientation in life, as well as the ability to develop as an individual.

However, if the necessity to conform is misused as a means for subordination, then emotional, creative, and headstrong life expressions are burdened with feelings of guilt or are socially outlawed or punished. Obstacles hindering further development stem from this, including narcissism and aggressiveness on the part of the individual and exploitation and lawlessness on the part of the collective group.

Wherever the segregating division between friend and foe emerges ("He who is not with me is against me"), totalitarianism and religious fundamentalism can be found lurking in the background.

It is no different in companies. A style of leadership characterized by mythical-conformist consciousness attempts to control untamed emotionality by means of rigid rules. The constructive step to establish common rules and limits becomes destructive if these rules are not managed with flexibility and if their original purpose corrupts into a regressive control system in which absolute loyalty, obedience, order, and respect are demanded.

Only weak managers place a great deal of emphasis on standards and conformity to secure their position, and in doing so they stifle the creativity of their employees.

Yet if the qualities of this consciousness level are recognized and applied to an appropriate degree, clarity and transparency in decision-making, as well as reliable rules that can be understood by everyone, are key prerequisites for creative work in the community. Rules are thus no longer applied in order to control and subordinate, but rather because they serve a larger cooperation. As a result, they can also be easily adapted to changing situations.

The expansion of the "I" beyond the mythical-conformist evolutionary stage led into the world of *rational-structuring consciousness*. The Reformation, which the conservative forces tried to suppress by means of the Spanish Inquisition, and the Renaissance paved the way; the Enlightenment gave rise to the radical demystification of the world and introduced a period of individual liberation and undreamed-of advances in science. The Industrial Age dawned, bringing with it health and prosperity for many. Absolutist forms of rule were replaced by democracy. The ideal of equal rights confronted slavery. Individualism and liberalism led away from the herd mentality and federal structures developed. Women began to fight for their rights and question the patriarchal order.

One-dimensional identification with this progress leads to the development of its dark sides; things one can see and measure become the absolute yardstick, reducing humans and the earth to a functioning machine.

The unfoldment of analytical, structuring ways of thinking gives the individual independence and power. Conventions that cannot be explained rationally are broken down and replaced by individual yardsticks. In the maturation process of human beings, this corresponds to becoming an adult.

In an integrated form, this rational development provides fairness, honesty, and equal opportunities for all.

The rational-structuring potential of the individual benefits companies in the form of goal-oriented strategies and structures. The myth of the "good patron" is replaced by the performance-conscious, ambitious manager. Career opportunities are no longer exclusively linked with social status. A broader basis of employees is involved in the decision-making processes.

However, the fascination with relentless technological development leads to the alienation of people from their environment. Whenever it is a matter of implementing goals, results, and strategies, of time management or of increasing efficiency or productivity, warning signals sent out by the body, feelings, and intuition are ignored, just as are the signs of the progressive destruction of the environment and of social cohesion.

The ideals that give the company its unique character and motivate the employees fall victim to the seduction of the doer by his excessive delusions of grandeur and greed, which result from this continual one-dimensional focus on maximizing productivity and efficiency. The ensuing long-term destruction of material corporate values is veiled.

In the Western industrialized nations, the protest against the destructive side of this mentality gave rise to alternative values in the 1960s, sparking a movement leading to the *rational-sensitive consciousness*, which moved away from egocentrism toward more compassion for the weak and more sensitive communication. Ecological concerns and respect for nature were focal points here, as was a growing understanding for cultural and religious plurality and for the fate of minorities. Human rights, liberation theology, ethics, and the protection of animals were also key issues in this consciousness phase.

The individual can perceive the effects of globalization. We are confronted with challenges that promote global thinking but which can also arouse fears for our own livelihood. We can find it difficult to come to terms with this broader sphere and the rapidly changing circumstances. The question as to the meaning of life is posed once again.

This sensitive rationality can form the transition to integral consciousness, provided that it does not become dogmatic. The dark side of this pluralistic consciousness lies in the fact that sensitivity for existing grievances and injustices, without perceiving them from a holistic viewpoint, can lead to the same one-sidedness that generated them. Condemnation and fanaticism cannot help remedy grievances, nor do they help find forward-looking solutions. Rather, the sensitive "I" regresses into the emotional trap of "either/or," into the rigid separation of good and evil that molds the behavior in the mythical consciousness. Responding to the lack of sensitive values in the world by means of the pent-up anger and power urges of the mythical-emotional consciousness, or by retreating into resignation, means a betrayal of the values we stand for. Thus it seems today that an entire generation of sensitive individuals, due to its protest/victim behavior, is locking itself out of the transition to a more all-encompassing perspective.

Because of their keen sense for discerning discrepancies, rational-sensitive people can often be a source of discomfort within a company. However, if a company succeeds in accepting and assimilating their criticism as a kind of creative tension between shortcomings and ideal situations, everyone wins: the consciousness and regeneration processes in the enterprise remain alive, while the "sensitives," who tend to take on the role of victim, gain a new understanding of personal responsibility within the community.

A corporation increasingly assumes social and ecological responsibility as soon as enough of its main actors have integrated the material, mythical, and rational consciousness levels. They are then so well acquainted with the elementary forces of these three spheres that they can use their respective potential to the benefit of the whole. At the same time, they are able to perceive things that irritate unconsciously, before they result in misinterpretations or wrong decisions.

In every community, people from all kinds of backgrounds and consciousness structures are brought together. Thus at all times, all levels of the consciousness evolution are present and working in different forms. Against this backdrop, the hierarchical company pyramid, with an "all-arounder" at the top, is no longer able to function. Broader expertise takes priority over power and status. Teamwork is encouraged. The doer becomes the shaper and has thereby already made the transition to *integral consciousness*.

Appendix B
Exercises

It might be useful to first record these exercises onto a cassette and play them back while you are meditating. Make sure that you leave long enough breaks between the individual elements.

<u>Preparatory Exercise: The Path to Silence</u>

- Sit comfortably on a chair with a firm seat, with your feet flat on the floor. By anchoring your sitting bones into the chair seat, you will feel your spine gently extending upward. Slightly draw your chin toward your breastbone so that the energy can flow freely up your spine and the back of your neck. You can either place your hands, with the forefinger and thumb touching, on your thighs or intertwine them so that your left hand rests in your right hand, with the tips of your thumbs touching. Close your eyes or let them rest on the floor in front of you.

- Now take a couple of deep breaths. On exhaling, successively relax your neck, shoulders, chest, back, arms and hands, pelvis, thighs, calves, and feet, right down to your toes.

- Inhale deeply and hold your breath. Detach from the notion of being in control and from holding on to anything in your muscles and joints. Let go of all the tension by exhaling deeply. Breathe normally again.

- Inhale deeply once again and hold your breath. Feel if any emotions of doubt, worry, or fear are stirring in your solar plexus. Let go of them by exhaling deeply. Breathe normally again.

- Take another deep breath and hold it. Detach from the activity of thinking and let go of your thoughts by exhaling deeply.

- Turn your awareness once again to the pulse of your breathing—of inhaling and exhaling—without consciously influencing it. If you notice that your thoughts are straying, gently return your awareness to your breathing, as it comes and goes.

- Continue to sit with this effortless awareness of your breathing. After a few minutes, you can either move on to another exercise or stay in this state of stillness. Try first of all to remain in this state of stillness for ten minutes, and gradually extend this period to twenty to thirty minutes.

Anchoring between Heaven and Earth

- Begin with the preparatory exercise (The Path to Silence).

- Imagine that your breath is flowing like a lead weight down through the base of your spine into the earth. As you inhale and exhale, feel yourself reaching deep down into the earth, like a tree taking root.

- When you feel that you are firmly anchored in the earth, with each outward breath, guide the energy of the earth up your back and let it flow through the top of your head into infinity. Imagine a crystal clear, intensive light high above you. Breathe the rising energy into this light. When you feel that you are firmly connected with this light, with every inward breath, allow the energy from this bright counter pole to flow through the middle of your head, down through your spine, and deep into the earth. Feel the two opposite flows of energy between heaven and earth as they continually move up (outward breath) and down (inward breath) your spine.

- When you can perceive this vertical flow, return to your breathing, being effortlessly aware of how it comes and goes.

- Now bring your attention to the inner area of your chest. Perhaps you can feel this area expanding, as if you were spreading out your arms. Breathe into this horizontally flowing energy current and perceive how with every outward breath, your chest expands a little more.

- When you can feel both the vertical and horizontal flows of your energy currents, return your awareness to your breathing. Horizontal and vertical energies cross in the region of your chest. The vertical flow serves to anchor you between heaven and earth. As it energizes your arms and hands, the horizontal flow represents the plane of human action in the world. Experience simultaneously your inner steadfastness and your readiness to act in the outside world. Continue to sit in this state or move on to the next exercise.

Finding the Witness

- Follow the Path of Silence and anchor yourself in the vertical plane. Be fully aware of the ever-new present moment.

- Effortlessly move your awareness to your body. How do you perceive it? Is your breath able to flow freely? Are you aware of being cold or hot anywhere in your body? Can you perceive pressure, tension, or pain? Whatever you perceive, encounter it with loving kindness and accept everything that is now. Allow any changes to take place without trying to hold on to them.

- Now gently shift your awareness to the emotional plane. What do you feel? Perceive your emotions, how they are, their intensity and dynamism. Accept what is. Remain in the present. Observe without judging. Be a loving witness to that which your inner emotions wish to express. Allow your inner emotions the space they require. At the same time, also accept any changes that take place, without trying to hold on to them.

- By slightly shifting your body and your awareness, step out of the activity of thinking. Observe your thoughts. Be aware of their movement and their intensity, without becoming involved in them. Do not hold on to your thoughts. Observe them lovingly; perceive changes without holding on to them.

- Who is the observer that is perceiving your body, emotions, and thoughts? If you were merely your body, in what way could you observe it? If you were no more than your thoughts and emotions, how could you witness them?

- Become aware of the space that surrounds the witness. Does it have a beginning or an end? How does it feel? Stay with it and surrender yourself to it. (We, as the witness, cannot willfully enter the space surrounding us. However, if we let go of all our intentions, the space may reach out and guide us in—into Oneness.)

Perceiving Solutions

- Think of an issue or question that would normally trigger your emotions or trouble your mind, and which you would like to resolve. Put it aside for the moment.

- Now enter the Path of Silence and anchor yourself in the vertical plane. Lovingly perceive the realms of your body, emotions, and thoughts, without judging them. Remain in the consciousness of the witness. Stay in the present and effortlessly be aware as you become still.

- Invite your chosen issue or question to appear in this realm of silence. Allow it to manifest itself in whatever form it chooses—as an image, a symbol, a color, or a physical or emotional presence. Accept this form of expression lovingly and without judgment. Continue to merely witness what manifests itself.

- Does that which you perceive trigger something within you? In your body, in your emotions, in your thoughts? Permit any impulses you may have. Put the chosen issue or question aside and turn your awareness to within yourself. Accept your reactions lovingly and give them space, without trying to hold on to them. By purely witnessing them, you allow them to transform themselves into stillness.

- From this tranquility, focus again on your issue or question. Embrace it with loving kindness. When you can bring it close to your heart in stillness, ask it what it wants to convey to you or requires of you—insight, behavior, concrete action, or simply awareness. Remain open and in the attitude of the loving witness. Perhaps you will perceive the answer as images or words, or in some other form of expression. It may even be that you do not perceive anything until you become aware of thinking, feeling, or acting differently when the issue or question next presents itself in your daily life.

- Remain in this state until you feel that you have taken in everything that is important to you. Then gently and gratefully detach yourself from all the images and messages. Bring your awareness back to your body; move it and perceive the room in which you are sitting.

- Reflect on what you have experienced and write it down. Have you understood the message? What effect will your inner perception have on the next practical steps you take?

Resolving Personal Relationships

- Is there someone around you with whom you would like to have a more constructive exchange or with whom you would like to interact in a more compassionate way, free of unconscious patterns that may mutually bind and limit you? Are you about to make an encounter for which you want to prepare yourself inwardly?

- Follow the Path of Silence and anchor yourself in the vertical plane. Perceive the realms of your body, emotions, and thoughts. Be a witness.

Remain aware of the present moment and let go of any impulses that may arise.

- Invite the person in question to appear before your inner eye. Accord this inner image the freedom it needs, as well as your respect.

- Sense if the image triggers reactions within you, whether physically, emotionally, or mentally. Turn your awareness to these resonances within you. Permit any impulses their intensity and the space they need. Witness what happens lovingly and acceptingly. Your loving kindness will allow the inner movements to transform themselves into stillness.

- From this tranquility, focus once more on the inner image of the person. Remain aware of the ever-new present and embrace it with loving kindness. Connect yourself with your inner wisdom and ask that the energy now needed by the person may flow to him or her through your heart. Surrender yourself to the process. Whatever happens will do so independently of your will. Do not force anything or try to hold on to anything.

- Stay with your heart in this state as long as you feel or have a presentiment of a flow of energy. Give thanks for this inner communication and slowly release yourself from the image. Bring your attention to your body. Move it, and go back to your everyday activities.

Harmonizing the Energy of a Company or Other Institution

- Follow the Path of Silence and anchor yourself in the vertical plane. Perceive the inner realms of your body, emotions, and thoughts. Be present and witness, without judging what you observe. Continually let go of all the impulses that may arise.

- Invite your company to appear as a subtle sphere between the hands of your open arms. Imagine your company as an energetic organism between your hands. Hold it with the loving kindness that is now flowing from your heart through your hands.

- Be aware of any reactions that may arise within you, whether physically, emotionally, or mentally. Allow these resonances, without identifying with them. Embrace every movement with the warmth of your heart and thus allow what you have witnessed to transform itself into stillness.

- Imagine that the sphere contains three further spheres, each encompassing the next.

- Focus on the innermost, smallest sphere. Imagine that it represents the physical plane of the company—that is, matter and life energy, health, and vitality. Touch the sphere with loving kindness. Remain aware of the present moment. Ask your inner wisdom what vibrational quality of heart energy this physical plane of the company requires from you and observe its flow in the form of tone, color, or pure energy. Remain open. Allow the sphere to absorb energy until it becomes light, round, and effortlessly maneuverable in all directions.

- Repeat the process with the two larger spheres. The smaller of the two represents the emotional plane—the charisma and power of attraction of the company. The second one refers to the rational plane, to the company's structured, goal-oriented way of thinking. Have trust in the inner wisdom that the energy quality required at the present moment will flow through your hands and that you will feel when the relevant sphere has absorbed sufficient energy, when it has become light, round, and easily maneuverable.

- Finally, perceive the outermost sphere, which encompasses the three smaller ones. It represents the spiritual dimension of the company. Observe how the company's spirit—its meaning or reason for existing— flows through the entire structure and saturates it.

- Release yourself gently from this experience and return to your everyday activities.

- During your next visit to the company, observe its subtle charisma. Treat it with loving kindness.

Appendix C
Recommended Books, Audio and Video Recordings, and Web sites

Avila, Teresa von. *Interior Castle*. New York: Image Books, 1972.

Barrett, Richard. *Liberating the Corporate Soul*. Woburn, MA: Butterworth, Heinemann, 1998.

Beck, Don Edward, and Christopher C. Cowan. *Spiral Dynamics: Mastering Values, Leadership and Change*. Oxford: Blackwell, 1996.

Brennan, Barbara. *Hands of Light*. New York: Random House, 1987.

Brook, Peter, director. *The Mahabharata*. DVD. USA, 2002.

Brook, Peter. *The Open Door*. New York: Random House, 1995.

Campbell, Joseph, and Bill Moyers. *The Power of Myth*. New York: Random House, 1991.

Dagar Brothers. *Raga Myian Ky Todi*. CD. Zurich, Switzerland: Jecklin, 1988.

Dagar, Ustad Faiyaz Wasifuddin. *The Art of Dagarvani Dhrupad—Nine Ragas of Night and Day*. 5 CDs. Zurich, Switzerland: Jecklin, 2000.

DeSoto, Hernando. *The Mystery of Capital: Why Capitalism Triumphs in the West and Fails Everywhere Else*. New York: Basic Books, 2000.

Diamond, John. *The Life Energy in Music*. Vol. 1. New York: Zeppelin, 1983.

Gebser, Jean. *The Ever-Present Origin*. Athens, OH: Ohio University Press, 1986.

Giok Liem, In. *Interdependent Economy: From Political Economy to Spiritual Economy*. Lincoln, NE: iUniverse, 2005.

Greenleaf, Robert K. *Servant Leadership: A Journey into the Nature of Legitimate Power and Greatness*. Mahwah, NJ: Paulist Press, 1983.

Gutzwiller, Andreas Fuyu, Shakuhachi. *The True Spirit of Emptiness*. CD. Zurich, Switzerland: Jecklin, 1987.

Harrison, Steven. *Doing Nothing: Coming to the End of the Spiritual Search*. East Rutherford, NJ: J. P. Tarcher, 2002.

Hertz, Norina. *The Silent Takeover: Global Capitalism and the Death of Democracy*. New York: Harper Business, 2001.

Inayat Khan, Hazrat. *The Mysticism of Sound and Music*. Boston, MA: Shambala, 1991.

Jung, Emma. *Animus and Anima*. New York: Continuum, 1985.

Landes, David S. *The Wealth and Poverty of Nations*. New York: W. W. Norton, 1998.

Laszlo, Ervin. *Macroshift: Navigating the Transformation to a Sustainable World*. San Francisco: Berrett Koehler, 2001.

Laszlo, Ervin. *Science and the Akashic Field*. Rochester, VT: Inner Traditions, 2004.

Maharshi, Ramana. *The Spiritual Teachings*. Boston, MA: Shambala, 1988.

Mann, Rudolf. *Das ganzheitliche Unternehmen*. Stuttgart, Germany: Schäfer Pöschel, 1995.

Mei-Ling Shyu. *Wechselbeziehung zwischen Musik und Politik in China und Taiwan*. Hamburg, Germany: 2001. www.sub.uni-hamburg.de/disse/454/ShyuDiss.pdf

Meister Eckhart. Vol. 1, *Teacher and Preacher*.

Vol. 2, *The Sermons*. Mahwah, NJ: Paulist Press, 1986.

Muktananda Paramahansa, Swami. *Where Are You Going?* South Fallsburg, NY: Siddha Yoga, 1994.

Narasimhan, C. V., trans. *The Mahabharata*. New York: Columbia University Press, 1997.

Neumann, Erich. *The Great Mother: An Analysis of the Archetype*. Princeton University Press, 1991.

Niasargadatta Maharaj, Sri. *I Am That*. Durham, NC: Acorn Press, 1990.

Odier, Daniel. *Tantric Quest: An Encounter with Absolute Love*. Rochester, VT: Inner Traditions, 1997.

Peck, Scott M. *The Different Drum: Community Making and Peace*. New York: Simon & Schuster, 1987.

Rawls, John. *A Theory of Justice*. Oxford: Oxford University Press, 1991.

Reiter, Peter. *Der Seele Grund: Meister Eckhart und die Tradition der Seelenlehre*. Würzburg, Germany: Königshausen & Neumann, 1993.

Saint-Exupéry, Antoine de. *The Wisdom of the Sands*. Chicago: University of Chicago Press, 1984.

Singh, Jaideva, trans. *Vijnana-Bhairava: The Yoga of Delight, Wonder, and Astonishment* Albany: State University of New York Press, 1991.

Singh, Jaideva, trans. *Spanda Karika: The Yoga of Vibration and Divine Pulsation*. Albany, NY: State University of New York Press, 1991.

Stiglitz, Joseph. *Globalization and Its Discontents* . New York: W. W. Norton, 2002.

Swimme, Brian. *The Universe Is a Green Dragon: A Cosmic Creation Story*. Rochester, VT: Bear & Co., 1984.

Swimme, Brian, and Thomas Berry. *The Universe Story: From the Primordial Flaring Forth to the Ecozoic Era—A Celebration of the Unfolding of the Cosmos.* San Francisco: HarperSanFrancisco, 1994.

Tame, David. *The Secret Power of Music.* Rochester, VT: Destiny Books, 1984.

Teilhard de Chardin, Pierre. *The Future of Man.* New York: Image Books, 2004.

Teilhard de Chardin, Pierre. *The Phenomenon of Man.* New York: HarperCollins, 1959.

Tolle, Eckart. *The Eckart Tolle Audio Series.* CD. Louisville, CO: Sounds True, 2002.

Tolle, Eckart. *The Power of NOW.* Novato, CA: New World Library, 1999.

Trio San José. *Ave Maria no morro, and others.* www.inselliste.de/triosanjose.html

Ulrich, Peter. *Facing Public Interest: Ethical Challenges to Business Policy and Corporate Communications.* Berlin, Germany: Kluwer Academic Publishers, 1995.

Wilber, Ken. *A Brief History of Everything.* Boston, MA: Shambala, 2001.

Wilber, Ken. *Cosmic Consciousness.* 10 CDs. Louisville, CO: Sounds True, 2003.

Wilber, Ken. *Integral Naked* (Web site). www.integralnaked.com

Wilber, Ken. *Integral Psychology: Consciousness, Spirit, Psychology, Therapy.* Boston, MA: Shambala, 2000.

Wilber, Ken. *One Taste.* Boston, MA: Shambala, 2000.

Wilber, Ken. *Sex, Ecology, Spirituality: The Spirit of Evolution.* Boston, MA: Shambala, 2001.

Wilber, Ken. *The Simple Feeling of Being: Visionary, Spiritual, and Poetic Writings.* Boston, MA: Shambala, 2004.

Wilhelm, Richard. *Frühling und Herbst des Lü Bu We.* Munich, Germany: Diederichs, 1979.

Wilhelm, Richard. *Li Gi: Das Buch der Riten, Sitten und Bräuche.* Munich, Germany: Diederichs, 1997.

Zur Bonsen, Matthias. *Führen mit Visionen.* Wiesbaden, Germany: Gabler, 1994.

978-0-595-35517-4
0-595-35517-X